BABY NAMES 2013

Ella Joynes

white
LADDER

Acknowledgements

I would like to extend my utmost gratitude to Cerys Owen, Shelley Heck, Michael Turner and Robin Boothroyd for their contributions; without them this book would have been much shorter. My thanks are also given to Beth Bishop and Jessica Spencer at Crimson Publishing for their patience and guidance throughout the project. Finally, the greatest thanks go to my children, Owen Henri and Jasper Hugh. I fall more in love with them and their names, every day.

This fourth edition published in Great Britain 2012 by
Crimson Publishing Ltd
Westminster House, Kew Road, Richmond, Surrey TW9 2ND

First, second and third editions published by Crimson Publishing in 2009, 2010 and 2011.

© Crimson Publishing, 2012

A catalogue record for this book is available from the British Library.

ISBN 978 1 90828 133 3

Typeset by IDSUK (DataConnection) Ltd
Printed and bound by L.E.G.O. S.p.A, Lavis TN

Contents

A note on how to use this book

While the author and publisher acknowledge that baby names vary widely in spelling and pronunciation, this book lists each name only once: under the most common initial and spelling. If a name has an alternative spelling with a different initial, it may be listed under that letter also.

Information relating to statistics and trends in baby names is based on the most recent data at the time of writing.

Introduction

Picking a name for your baby is one of the most enjoyable activities for a new parent, but it's also one of the most daunting. Sometimes choosing the right name is simply a case of hearing one you like and knowing instantly that you've chosen correctly. But, for the vast majority of parents the naming game gets far more complicated when you start trying to please parents, grandparents, friends, and siblings, while trying to avoid names that could be shortened into ridiculous nicknames or would make for funny initials.

You'll also probably want to choose something unique, but not *too* unique, or something common, but not *too* common. A name could be inspired by an admired celebrity, a sports star, or an influential historical or political figure. It could also come from the family tree, or follow a current baby-naming trend. You also need to make sure you love it – you'll have to live with it forever! The possibilities are endless so it's understandable that it can set some parents into panic mode.

Well, never fear. *Baby Names 2013* is here to take you through your options and solve your baby-naming dilemmas. It's updated annually, so it always includes the year's most popular names, celebrity choices, and names making a comeback. We've included dozens of lists to provide you with inspiration, and, of course, some downright weird names children have been given over the years (usually by celebs).

Take a peek at the most up-to-date trends in baby-naming, from the backlash against quirky names to the return of the traditional, and some recent celebrity trends. Read about how the latest developments in the Space Race could impact baby names, what movie characters you'll want to name your baby after, and what names make for the cleverest kids . . .

Be sure to also keep an eye out for all the facts and figures we've got for you – including what names are most popular around the world – so you can either go with the flow . . . or deliberately against it.

The average length of a baby name is six letters.

This book is broken into two sections: the first deals with how to figure out what to name your child through a series of questions and suggestions, and the second gives you a meaning for each name you're considering. There's no right or wrong way to use this book, just as there's no right or wrong way to make your baby-naming decision.

Remember, picking a baby name should be fun – so dip in, find some names you like, and use the suggestions we've given you to work out if one of them is a winner!

part one

1

What was hot in 2012?

Look-alikes and sound-alikes: Oliver and Olivia

In 2012 the most popular names for baby boys and baby girls were Oliver and Olivia. It's remarkable that two such similar-sounding names are topping the charts, but the fact they share a meaning shouldn't surprise anyone (they're both of Latin origin and mean 'olive' or 'olive tree', unsurprisingly). They were also the two most popular names the year before, which suggests the reign of Jack is officially over (Jack held the boys' top spot for a whopping 14 years before 2011). The fastest climbers in 2012 were Lacey for girls (up 31 places to position 36) and Zachary for boys (in at position 51 after a jump of 16 places), while the names Aidan, Callum, Isobel, and Libby all fell out of favour and dropped by at least 12 places each.

For girls' names there were no new entries at all to the Top 10, and the only change in the line-up for boys' names was George, which replaced Daniel, and moved from position 11 last year to number nine. There were also only six new names in the Top 100 boys' names (Bobby, Caleb, Dexter, Jensen, Kayden, and Ollie), and another six newcomers in the girls' list (Aisha, Annabelle, Eliza, Laila, Maryam, and Maisy). This is a similar case to the previous year, which only saw six new boys' names and three new girls' names, and suggests that parents are once again returning to more familiar and widely-used names and spellings.

Names to drop out of the Top 100 completely were Alisha, Eve, Francesca, Lydia, and Sara for girls, and Austin, Christopher, Ellis, Ewan, Joe, and Morgan for boys. However, it's also interesting to look at how names were chosen during the different months of the year: while Oliver remained first in 11 months of last year, it was overtaken by Harry in November. Likewise, Olivia was top for 10 months of the year but Lily claimed the crown in November, and that classic Christmas favourite, Holly, was first in December. Holly never gets the top spot in June and July . . .

So, what baby names were popular last year?

Top 10 baby names

Boys	Girls
1. Oliver	1. Olivia
2. Jack	2. Sophie
3. Harry	3. Emily
4. Alfie	4. Lily
5. Charlie	5. Amelia
6. Thomas	6. Jessica
7. William	7. Ruby
8. Joshua	8. Chloe
9. George	9. Grace
10. James	10. Evie

> " All British people have plain names, and that works pretty well over there. "
>
> Paris Hilton

The end of quirky names?

Around the turn of the millennium an interesting phenomenon took place: only 50% of babies born in the UK had their names represented in the Top 50 baby names list. This meant that for over 10 years 50% of all British babies were given such unique and diverse names that they were not common enough to get listed on the national rankings. This included variations in spellings too, as the Office for National Statistics uses the exact spelling listed on a birth certificate for its calculations.

However, in 2012 this wave of originality seemed to lose its swell. Of the 700,000 babies who had their live births registered, over half of them saw their names appear in the Top 100 – and more of those than ever were in the Top 50. Spelling does have an impact on statistics, though, as two similar-sounding names are always listed separately. To make this clearer, if one child were called Lily (ranked eighth in 2011 and fourth in 2012) and another were called Lilly (ranked 45th in 2011 and 39th in 2012), they would still be ranked separately to their classmates Lili and Lillie (neither of which ranked in the Top 100 of either year). However, the fact that both Lily and Lilly jumped in the charts last year, and the less well-known variations of Lili and Lillie did not, shows the newest fashion for parents to pick familiar and traditional names.

This trend is seen over and over again in 2012 statistics: more traditional names, such as Noah, look like they are making big gains (up 14 places to position 18 at the time of writing), while unusual names, such as Maddison (spelt with two 'd's instead of the traditional one), fell in popularity. It's possible that celebrities are partially responsible for this new way of thinking, which is discussed in more detail on page 12.

Some of Britain's quirky baby names during the last year have included Goldy, La, and Rejoice for a girl, and Bakery, Twin, and Zyan for a boy.

The Top 10 for both boys and girls has been made up of pretty much the same names for the last seven years. It seems that although some parents like to be adventurous in their choice of name, many pick one for their child that doesn't have any quirky or weird connotations, thereby avoiding any possible assumptions people may make about an unusual name.

Names such as Alfie, Archie, Harry, Maisie, and Harriet had dropped out of mainstream use by the 1970s and became vastly unpopular, but in the last few years names ending in -a, -ie, and -y have started to see a resurgence, particularly as a spelling option for parents who like the sound of a traditional name but want to give it a modern twist. Other old-fashioned names, such as Arthur, Ava, Florence, and Sebastian, have climbed the popularity ranks in the Top 100 lists, joining such stalwarts as Alexander, Alice, Grace, and Thomas.

The traditional Muslim name Mohammed has now become so popular in the UK that if just the three spelling variations in the Top 100 were counted as the same name, it would be the fourth most popular name for baby boys in the country. The spelling 'Mohammed' is the most common (ranked 17th), followed by 'Muhammad' (31st), and 'Mohammad' (67th). However, since last year the spelling 'Mohammed' has dropped in popularity in certain parts of the country. In 2011 it was the most popular baby boy's name in the West Midlands, and the fourth most popular in London, but in 2012 it dropped to fourth position in the West Midlands and fifth in London.

❝❝ Each generation wants new symbols, new people, new names. They want to divorce themselves from their predecessors. ❞❞

Jim Morrison

2012's fastest-climbing names

Boys	Girls
Jude	Esme
Kai	Florence
Noah	Lacey
Zachary	Maisie

. . . but we still love originality

It's probably unfair to say that all parents are reverting back to traditional names, as a simple analysis of last year's baby name statistics suggest otherwise. Names with quirks, twists, surprising spellings, and lashings of originality are still being chosen by families throughout the year. One of the most common ways parents are putting a twist on tradition is by hyphenating their daughters' names. At the time of writing in 2012, the most often-reported hyphens were -Rose, -May/-Mae, and -Leigh/-Lee, with over 1,000 names having these tacked on to the end of another name: some examples include Ellie-May (205th), Lily-Mae (214th), Lily-Rose (268th), and Demi-Leigh (422nd). Individually these may not seem like high-ranking positions, but if you add all the spelling variations together, names that end in May or Mae would be in the Top 20 for the first time, and those that include Rose would be around position 50!

Top 10 names in Australia

Boys	Girls
1. Oliver	1. Chloe
2. Noah	2. Sophie
3. William	3. Ruby
4. Lachlan	4. Charlotte
5. Ethan	5. Olivia
6. Jack	6. Lily
7. Lucas	7. Ava
8. Charlie	8. Ella
9. Joshua	9. Emily
10. Thomas	10. Mia

For boys, giving a baby a shortened version of a traditional name as his complete first name is becoming increasingly popular. For example, at the time of writing, the most popular name for little boys was Oliver. Shortened versions of this have now climbed the ranks as well: Ollie sits in position 63, and Olly appears at 113. The name James has often appeared in the Top 10, and last year its nickname Jamie slotted in at position 49. This has also happened with William (ranked 7th): Billy is 101st, Will is 234th, and Wil appears further down. Surprisingly though, the names 'Willy' and 'Willie' weren't given to a single child last year in the entire United Kingdom! I wonder why . . .

In opposition to previous years, 2012 has definitely seen a slow-down in terms of quirky names and spellings. However, it's clear there are still large numbers of parents designing their own spellings and variations, because so far (in 2012) there have been 5,707 different baby girl names registered and 4,678 baby boy names. This means that there are 10,385 completely unique names out there, and some incredibly creative parents!

A selection of last year's original spellings for girls include Maariya (from the more common Maria), Emilee (from Emily), Loren (from Lauren), and Caci, Casie, Casy, Kacey, Kaci, Kacy, and Kasie (from the most common spelling of Casey). Boys' names variations included Tomass (from Thomas), Troi (from Troy), Salomon (from Solomon), and Michail, Micheel, Michel, Mickael, Miikyle, and Mikkel (from Michael).

Colin Firth doesn't like his name, apparently. In 2011 he was quoted as saying: 'Colin is the sort of name you'd give your goldfish for a joke. I once saw an episode of Blackadder with a dachshund in it called Colin. It seemed his name alone was supposed to reduce you to fits of laughter.'

The cult of celebrity

As always, the celebrity world continues to influence choices made by parents in 2012 – but we have seen a distinct return to more traditional names.

Names beginning with 'A' are massively popular with celebrities at the moment. Names such as Agnes (Jennifer Connelly and Paul Bettany's daughter), Aleph (Natalie Portman and Benjamin Millepied's son), Arthur (both

Claudia Winkleman and Selma Blair chose this for their sons), and Arlo (Johnny Knoxville's son) were fairly big hits with non-celebrities too: Arthur appears in position 82, and even Agnes, which hasn't been seen in the Top 1,000 since before the year 2000, claimed position 758.

Although celebrities are often known for choosing highly original (or simply weird) names for their children, new arrivals in the last year or so have actually been given fairly normal names by their standards. However, there is definitely a trend for choosing old-fashioned names – celebrities are certainly showing they're not afraid of names which the world hasn't used widely since the Second World War. Baby girls were named Delilah (Kimberley Stewart and Benicio Del Toro), Hattie (Tori Spelling and Dean McDermott), Ethel (Lily Allen and Sam Cooper), and Mabel Ray (Bruce Willis and Emma Heming Willis). In the case of Tori Spelling, it's claimed she picked all the names of her children according to people who'd been influential in her life – for daughter Hattie Margaret, this meant being named after Spelling's childhood nanny. Now Spelling has announced her fourth pregnancy (due in September 2012), it will be interesting to see what name she chooses this time around.

Baby boys were not exempt from the old-fashioned rule though: names chosen by celebrity parents of baby boys in 2011 and 2012 included Samuel (Jennifer Garner and Ben Affleck), Henry (Emily Deschanel and David Hornsby), and Eugene Pip (Billie Piper and Laurence Fox). In the case of Billie Piper and Laurence Fox, their choice of name seems to have a great deal of family significance – Eugene's middle

name is both a nod to the character of Pip in Dickens'
Great Expectations (a recording of which Laurence Fox
made for Classic FM recently), and to the fact Billie Piper
shares her name with Fox's mother's maiden name (both
are Piper).

Celebrity babies of 2011/2012

Arlo (Johnny Knoxville and Naomi Nelson, Oct 2011)

Giulia (Carla Bruni-Sarkozy and Nicholas Sarkozy,
Oct 2011)

Hattie Margaret (Tori Spelling and Dean McDermott,
Oct 2011)

Tristan Milos (Vanessa and Donald Trump Jr, Oct 2011)

Mason Evan (Monyetta Shaw and Ne-Yo, Oct 2011)

Lourdes (Alex and Steven Gerrard, Nov 2011)

Ace Billy (Matt and Emma Willis, Nov 2011)

Ethel Mary (Lily Allen and Sam Cooper, Nov 2011)

Elise (Celia Walden and Piers Morgan, Nov 2011)

Hollie Rose (Amanda Holden and Chris Hughes,
Jan 2012)

Kaya Emory (Lindsay Davenport and Jonathan Leach,
Jan 2012)

Blue Ivy (Beyoncé Knowles and Jay Z, Jan 2012)

Romy Hero (Sam Taylor-Wood and Aaron Johnson,
Jan 2012)

Exton Elias (Susan and Robert Downey Jr, Feb 2012)

Estelle Silvia Ewa Mary (Sweden's Crown Princess
Victoria and Prince Daniel, Feb 2012)

Samuel (Jennifer Garner and Ben Affleck, Mar 2012)

Aoife Belle (Una Healy and Ben Foden, Mar 2012)

Jackson (Charlize Theron, adopted Mar 2012)

Luca Cruz (Hilary Duff and Eric Comrie, Mar 2012)

Hunter (Sarah Cawood and Andy Merry, Mar 2012)

Covey (Konnie Huq and Charlie Brooker, Mar 2012)

Eugene Pip (Billie Piper and Laurence Fox, Apr 2012)

Mabel Ray (Bruce Willis and Emma Heming Willis,
    Apr 2012)

Pearl (Jack Osbourne and Lisa Stelly, Apr 2012)

Ray (Sophie Ellis-Bextor and Richard Jones, Apr 2012)

Astala (Peaches Geldof and Thomas Cohen, Apr 2012)

Gloria Ray (Maggie Gyllenhaal and Peter Sarsgaard,
    April 2012)

Leighton (Stacey Solomon and Aaron Barham,
    May 2012)

Keeva (Alyson Hannigan and Alexis Denisof,
    May 2012)

In the US charts, the name Elvis dropped out of the Top 1,000 US baby names in 2010, the first year it had not made the list since 1954.

Of course, celebrities were not entirely sensible last year and there was the usual selection of unique and odd-sounding names that we have come to love and expect. Beyoncé and husband Jay Z have chosen perhaps the wackiest name for their daughter: Blue Ivy. According to the media, 'Blue' was chosen because it's daddy Jay Z's favourite colour; 'Ivy' has several proposed meanings, starting with the fact it looks like the Roman number IV, which means '4'. The number four is significant to the couple for several reasons – they were married on 4/4 (4 April), they both have birthdays on the fourth of the month, and Beyoncé's fourth album was called, inspiringly, '4'. Shame they didn't keep it for their fourth child really . . .

Numbers as names didn't escape other celebrity couples either: Victoria and David Beckham gave their highly-anticipated daughter Harper the middle name Seven. For more on middle name trends, see page 53.

Beyoncé might be on to something: Blue Ivy is the sixth celebrity child to be named after the colour. Other 'blue' parents include Cher, John Travolta, The Edge, Geri Halliwell, and Alicia Silverstone.

Mariah Carey and Nick Cannon's twins followed the trend of wacky celebrity baby names – baby girl Monroe was named after Marilyn Monroe, and Moroccan Scott was named after the Moroccan Room in his parent's penthouse, where Nick proposed, and Scott is Nick's middle name. Mariah sent fans into a frenzy when she strung her name announcement out for hours, getting her followers on Twitter to guess the names from her clue.

Wacky celebrity baby names of recent years

Bingham Hawn (Kate Hudson and Matthew Bellamy – also parents to Ryder)

Bluebell Madonna (Geri Halliwell)

Blue Ivy (Beyonce Knowles and Jay Z)

Bronx Mowgli (Ashlee Simpson and Pete Wentz)

Buddy Bear Maurice (Jules and Jamie Oliver – also parents to Daisy Boo, Poppy Honey, and Petal Blossom Rainbow)

Cosima Violet (Claudia Schiffer and Matthew Vaughn – also parents to Caspar and Clementine)

Dixie Dot (Anna Ryder Richardson)

Egypt Dauode Dean (Alicia Keys and Swizz Beatz)

Ever Imre (Alanis Morissette and Mario Treadway)

Harper Seven (Victoria and David Beckham – also parents to Brooklyn, Romeo, and Cruz)

Ickhyd (M.I.A. and Ben Brewer)

Kahekili (Evangeline Lilly and Norman Kali)

Moses (Gwyneth Paltrow and Chris Martin – also parents to Apple)

Shiloh Nouvel (Brad Pitt and Angelina Jolie – also parents to Zahara, Maddox, Pax, Knox, and Vivienne)

Sparrow (Nicole Richie and Joel Madden – also parents to Harlow Winter)

Spike (Mike Myers and Kelly Tisdale)

Sunday Rose (Nicole Kidman and Keith Urban)

Zuma Nesta Rock (Gwen Stefani and Gavin Rossdale – also parents to Kingston)

The impact of characters in TV shows, movies, and books has been having a huge impact on baby names in the last few years. In 2012 the film based on the novel *The Hunger Games* provided parents with a whole host of alternative spellings for already popular names. We expect the names Peeta and Gale, for example, to enter the boys' names lists for the first time ever, and it's only a matter of time (and two more movies) before Katniss herself becomes an influence on girls' names. The name Primrose, or 'Prim', has started to climb the charts too, which supports the idea that parents are starting to choose old-fashioned names again.

Other influential books and TV programmes include *Scott and Bailey*, whose main characters Rachel Bailey and Janet Scott saw their names slightly move ahead in the charts – Bailey, in particular, was popular for baby boys and landed at position 79. The third series of *Downton Abbey* also continued to impress parents: the name Violet for example, from Maggie Smith's acerbic character The Right Honourable Violet Crawley, Countess of Grantham, has proved the most popular: nearly 500 baby girls were given the name Violet last year.

For more on influential pop culture, see page 27.

An Israeli couple have called their baby girl 'Like' after the Facebook button. Their other children are called Pie and Vash, which means honey.

Banned names around the world

@ – China

Akuma (meaning 'devil') – Japan

Anus – Denmark

Chow Tow (meaning 'smelly head') – Malaysia

Dalmata (meaning 'Dalmatian') – Italy

Gesher (meaning 'bridge') – Norway

Monkey – Denmark

Ovnis (meaning 'UFO') – Portugal

Q – Sweden

Sor Chai (meaning 'insane') – Malaysia

Stompy – Germany

2

What does 2013 hold for baby names?

Will these trends continue?

Looking forward to 2013, the trend for choosing either old-fashioned or unique names for babies seems set to continue.

It is also likely that parents will continue the trend of naming their children shortened versions of longer, more traditional names. The name Maisie (14th last year), for example, is a shortened version of Margaret (505th), while Leo (36th) and Leon (60th) are shorter versions of Leonardo (256th) and Leonard (413th) – these shorter names are clearly more popular than the longer ones. Other boys' names that are overtaking their longer namesakes include

Bobby, which is the shortened form of Robert. Last year Bobby jumped a massive 21 places to position 83, and has seen a huge increase in popularity in the last 10 years; it has climbed 190 places in a decade. Robert, on the other hand, has moved down 49 places in the same timespan and now sits in 90th place.

It isn't just for boys, either. Girls' names have begun to experience a similar effect: the traditional names Elizabeth and Eleanor have many nicknames, and last year several of these appeared higher up the charts than their full-length inspirations. Elizabeth sits at position 49 and Eleanor is at 69, but Ella claims the 18th spot and Ellie is 29th. In fact, while Elizabeth and Eleanor have both dropped in popularity over the last decade, Ella has made slow but steady progress in the opposite direction. It's now so common that it is more often seen as a name in its own right than a derivative of another. For more on this trend see page 11.

Predicted Top 10 baby names in 2013

Boys	Girls
1. Oliver	1. Olivia
2. Jack	2. Sophie
3. Harry	3. Lily
4. Charlie	4. Amelia
5. Alfie	5. Emily
6. Thomas	6. Jessica
7. William	7. Ruby
8. Joshua	8. Chloe
9. George	9. Evie
10. James	10. Grace

2013 events

Other influences on the names parents choose in 2013 may come from the worlds of sport, politics, and celebrity.

After the hugely publicised London Olympics and Paralympics in 2012, sporting events in 2013 seem a little tame by comparison. However, for football fans there is the 2013 Africa Cup of Nations in South Africa and the UEFA Women's Euro in Sweden, the athletic World Championships in Moscow, and the Rugby League World Cup, which the UK will be co-hosting this time around.

Rugby league players have often influenced baby names in the past, and there's no reason why 2013 should prove to be any different. In fact, after New Zealand's win in the 2008 Rugby League World Cup, several of the players' and coaches' names jumped in popularity. And, after the upset caused by the 2008 final, the games between Australia and New Zealand in particular will prove excellent food for thought for new parents.

The Olympics and Paralympics proved how inspirational great sporting stars can be. It stands to reason that the heroes of great games inspire some parents to name their children after them, and we were not disappointed. Past Olympic winners for Great Britain have included Steve Redgrave, Kelly Holmes, and Amir Khan, and, as these three athletes mentored 2012 contenders, their success was reflected in baby names statistics. Jessica Ennis, the track and field athlete, saw her name placed 6th on the charts last year, and even the mastermind behind the successful

London bid, Sir Sebastian Coe, saw his name jump four places in the charts to 58th.

One major set of events planned for 2013 is more space exploration. The People's Republic of China will launch its first unmanned space flight to the Moon, and the USA is sending a new explorer to Mars, called MAVEN, and another to Venus. It's a possibility that key players in these events will become famous, which will undoubtedly affect baby name statistics.

2013 will also be a fairly important year politically. At the time of writing the USA's presidential election had not taken place, but whatever the outcome and whomever the President is as of 1 January 2013, it is sure to be the result of a bitter and hard-won political battle. Politicians have a hazy history of influencing baby names – it's not true to say that children are frequently named after presidents or prime ministers, but there are exceptions. President Barack Obama's name has yet to enter even the Top 1,000 in the USA, and David Cameron's first name has dropped 22 places in the last 10 years. However, David Cameron's *last* name has appeared in the Top 100 pretty consistently over the last 20 years, and shows no sign of dropping out in the near future.

Interestingly though, there is a trend of naming babies after the *children* of politicians – Barack Obama's daughters are named Maliyah and Sasha, and a variation of both of these appear in the USA's Top 100 names for girls. When David Cameron's newborn daughter was named Florence in 2010, the media went wild, and a flurry of parents started choosing this name for their baby girls shortly after. In fact, it jumped an astonishing 26 places the year she was born, and has moved up 108 in the last 10 years. Even Florrie, which is a popular nickname for Florence, has appeared in the charts for the first time ever.

Don't forget to register your baby's birth! Labour leader Ed Miliband came under scrutiny when he didn't register his first son's birth in 2009. As he and his partner, Justine Thornton, weren't then married, Miliband was supposed to attend the registration with her so he could be listed as the baby's father, but neglected to do so. (He was present at the registration of his second son's birth in November 2010 though.)

2013 anniversaries

Significant anniversaries can potentially influence baby names. In 2013 this includes the 10th anniversary of British Sign Language being recognised as an official language of Great Britain (as first established by Thomas Braidwood in the 18th century), the 40th anniversary of the UK's admittance to the European Community (now called the European Union or EU), the 150th anniversary of the London Underground's first connection, the 200th year since Jane Austen's *Pride and Prejudice* was published, and 225 years since *The Times* first made it to our newsstands, under the direction of founder John Walter.

Other anniversaries include 25 years since the Lockerbie bombing, the 40th anniversary of Concorde's first non-stop flight across the Atlantic (and the 10th anniversary of their last . . .), the 50th anniversary of the Great Train Robbery, 50 years since the BBC first broadcast an episode of *Doctor Who*, starring William Hartnell and Carole Ann Ford, 125 years since The Football League was founded, 125 years since Jack the Ripper first struck, the 175th anniversary of the coronation of Queen Victoria, the 400th year since the original Globe Theatre burned to the ground, and 600 years since Henry V took to the throne with his wife Catherine of Valois.

A significant anniversary year for women's rights, 2013 includes the 100th anniversary of UK suffragette Emily Davison's death (she was killed by jumping in front of the King's horse), the 100th anniversary of all women's suffrage in Norway, and 130 years since New Zealand granted every woman the right to vote (thanks to women such as Kate Sheppard and Mary Ann Müller). It's also been 50 years since Afghanistan, Iran, Kenya, and Morocco each allowed equal political rights to women.

Don't be surprised, therefore, if names linked to these anniversaries start becoming popular. As the media at large begins to broadcast these significant dates, names such as Thomas (Braidwood), Jane (Austen), Elizabeth (Bennet), Darcy, John (Walter), Jack (the Ripper), Carole Ann (Ford), Emily (Davison), Kate (Sheppard), Mary Ann (Müller), Victoria (Queen), Henry (King), Catherine (of Valois), and William (Shakespeare and Hartnell) will start to be considered by parents as potential options for their baby names. And, the more heavily they're promoted, the more frequently they'll be used.

2013 anniversary names

Boys	Girls
Austen	Carole Ann
Bennet	Catherine
Darcy	Elizabeth
Henry	Emily
Jack	Kate
John	Jane
Thomas	Mary Ann
William	Victoria

The influence of pop culture

Pop culture will be perhaps the most prominent influence on baby names in the coming year. Celebrity couples expecting babies in late 2012 and in 2013 include Reese Witherspoon, Uma Thurman, and a Take That hat-trick: Mark Owen, Gary Barlow, and Robbie Williams. If the choices of names these celebrities make are particularly noteworthy, they may well influence the choices made by the general population. For more on how celebrity baby names affect current trends, see page 12.

"Words have meaning and names have power**"**

Anonymous

Expected new arrivals in 2012/2013

Mark and Emma Owen (July 2012)

Natalie Anderson and James Shepherd (Aug 2012)

Shilpa Shetty and Raj Kundra (Summer 2012)

Vanessa and Nick Lachey (Summer 2012)

Kristin Cavallari and Jay Cutler (Summer 2012)

Neve Campbell and JJ Field (Summer 2012)

Drew Barrymore and Will Kopelman
    (unconfirmed – Autumn 2012)

Reese Witherspoon and Jim Toth
    (unconfirmed – Autumn 2012)

Frank Skinner and Cath Mason (Autumn 2012)

Uma Thurman and Arpad Busson (Autumn 2012)

Gary and Dawn Barlow (Autumn 2012)

Robbie Williams and Ayda Field (Autumn 2012)

Nicole 'Snooki' Polizzi and Jionni LaValle (Autumn 2012)

Sarah Michelle Geller and Freddie Prince Jnr (Autumn/
    Winter 2012)

Tori Spelling and Dean McDermott (Sept 2012)

Anna Paquin and Stephen Moyer (Autumn 2012)

Adele and Simon Konecki (Autumn 2012/2013)

What's exciting about pop culture is how everything, from films and TV to books and blogs, can shape the world of baby names.

The year 2013 looks set to be the year of the remake, reboot, and sequel. Upcoming movies in 2013 include a new instalment in the Wizard of Oz franchise, *Oz: The*

Great and Powerful; a new Superman movie, *Superman: Man of Steel*; the next episode in Stieg Larsson's Girl trilogy, *The Girl Who Played With Fire*; another Lara Croft sequel; *Iron Man 3*; *The Smurfs 2*; *Despicable Me 2*; *Scary Movie 5*; and new versions of *Dirty Dancing, Robocop, Teenage Mutant Ninja Turtles*, and *Jurassic Park*. It will also be the year of the classic fairy tale, with *Hansel and Gretel: Witch Hunters, Jack the Giant Killer* and a new Disney movie called *King of the Elves* in the works.

It's likely that *Oz: The Great and Powerful* will be a massive hit, and its stars – James Franco, Mila Kunis, Rachel Weisz, and Michelle Williams – will also be in huge demand in 2013. However, because the character of Dorothy isn't actually in this film (it's a prequel to *The Wizard of Oz*), that name will probably not have as big an impact as it did in 1939 when the original was released. At that time it was the 9th most popular girl's name, but has since dropped to 695th place. Perhaps the name Oz will become a sudden runaway success this time around? (Only four baby boys were given that name last year though, so perhaps not. . .)

It's great when movie studios release films that are remakes and sequels, because you can look back at when the original versions were released and see how baby name trends were affected at the time. For example, when the original *Lara Croft: Tomb Raider* movie was released in 2001, the name Lara jumped an impressive 100 places in a single year. Last year it sat at position 124, so it's entirely possible it will appear in the Top 100 for the first time in over a decade once the new film is released. The same can be said of the characters in Steig Larsson's Girl trilogy:

in Sweden, the name Mikael has been steadily growing in popularity over the last five years, so it will be interesting to see what happens next. (Incidentally, if you want to take a look at how other countries around the world display their baby name statistics, I highly recommend starting with Sweden's official website. I have yet to find a country that presents its figures in a clearer or user-friendlier format.)

If you need inspiration, why not try following the latest trend from the USA and consider a character from your favourite book or film? The names Edward, Isabella, and Jacob have all leapt in popularity since the release of *Twilight* by Stephenie Meyer, and Isabella now tops the charts for baby girls. Even surnames of these characters have increased in popularity: the name Cullen jumped 300 places in a single year.

The final instalment of the *Twilight* phenomenon, *Breaking Dawn: Part II*, was released in 2012, and like the Harry Potter series before it, it demonstrated just how powerful pop culture can be. Isabella continued to be the favourite baby girl name in the USA and held 12th position in the UK, and the Cullens' daughter, called Renesmee, saw her name introduced to the charts for the first time. It's entirely possible that this influence will continue to grow, too. As the teenagers of today start to grow up and have children themselves, we may see more babies being named after *Twilight* characters – even 10 or 15 years from now.

Popular TV programmes set to air in 2013 include the third series of the popular *Sherlock*, and the final series of the hit show *Skins*. There is also likely to be another *Doctor Who* series airing in 2013, as well as a potential new series of *The Only Way is Essex* and *Made in Chelsea*. So watch out for new baby names hitting the headlines, such as Sherlock (*Sherlock*), Franky (*Skins*), Alo (*Skins*), Lydia (TOWIE), Caggie (*Made in Chelsea*), Arg (TOWIE). Also look out for the new companions for *Doctor Who* – no guesses yet as to their names, but they're worth watching out for.

Rising stars

Boys	Girls
Alo	Gretel
Arg	Lydia
Hansel	Lara
Jack	Caggie
Mikael	Lisbeth
Sherlock	Renesmee

3

How to choose a name

Top tips on choosing a name

- **Fall in love with the name(s) you've chosen.** If you
  plough through hundreds of names in this book and
  none of them jump off the page at you, then you
  probably haven't found the right one yet. Likewise, if
  a relative, friend, or even your spouse suggests a name
  and you wrinkle your nose every time you hear it, it's
  not the name for your baby. You should pick a name that
  you can shout with confidence across the schoolyard,
  or hear with pride when they graduate from university.
  Pick a name that makes you smile because if you love it,
  hopefully your child will too.

- **Don't listen to other people.** Sometimes, grandparents and friends will offer 'advice' during this time which may not always be welcome. This is worth bearing in mind if you've fallen in love with a name and it's either slightly unusual or doesn't follow the set pattern your partner's family have used for the last 50 years. Sharing your choice of name with other people can lead them to criticise it, which you'd probably rather not hear if you've got your heart set on it. Also, if you're bucking with tradition and don't plan on calling your newborn after their great-great-great-grandfather, keeping it a secret until after the birth and registration can work to your advantage. Trust your own instincts and remember: no one will really care once they see your baby. Its name will simply be its name.

- **Find a name with meaning.** When my parents discovered they were expecting a baby, they sought out possibilities that *meant* something. Both interested in history, they eventually settled on naming their three daughters after Queens of England (Alexandra, Eleanor and Victoria), hoping to fill their children's souls with a sense of pride and importance. It worked, because throughout our lives we have all felt a duty to do our names justice in the modern world – although I now use the name Ella more frequently than Eleanor. Having a name that has a back story helps your child understand their significance in the world, so whether you name them after a saint or prophet, an important political figure or a hero in a Greek tragedy, ensure they know where their name came from. They may just be inspired to be as great as their namesake.

- **Have fun.** Picking out names should be a fun process. Laughing at the ones you'd never dream of choosing can really help you narrow it down to the ones you would. You can also experiment with different spellings, pronunciations, or variations of names you like, or go to places where you might feel inspired. Some of the best names come from the worlds of nature and literature, so why not go down to your local garden centre or library and have fun with the classic, cute, and downright silly words you find there?

- **Expand your mind.** Don't rule out the weird ones just yet! As a teenager I went to school with a girl named Siam. Her parents had conceived her on a honeymoon trip to Thailand and given her the country's old name as a result. She loved growing up and having an unusual name, as I'm sure Lourdes (Stephen and Alex Gerrard's daughter) and Egypt (Alicia Keys and Swizz Beatz's son) do too. Also, don't be afraid to play around with spellings and pronunciations, even if the results are a little less than conformist. The name Madison, for example, could be spelt Maddison, Madyson, Maddiesun, or even Maddeesunn if you so choose, although you might want to be careful you don't saddle your child with an impossible name to spell, pronounce *and* fit on a passport application form.

- **Try it out.** While you're pregnant, talk to your baby and address it using a variety of your favourite names to see if it responds. There are numerous stories of names being chosen because the baby kicked when it was called Charlie or Aisha, but was suspiciously silent when it was called Dexter or Mildred, so see if it has a preference! You can also try writing names down and sticking them to your fridge, or saying one out loud enough times to see if you ever get sick of it. That name you picked out when you were eight and always said you'd name your first child, for example, might not sound so appropriate now you're an adult and have to name a human being for real.

- **Do NOT pick the name of an ex.** No matter how lovely Brad Pitt thought the name 'Jennifer' was, it's unlikely Angelina Jolie would have allowed him to use it for one of their daughters. The same is probably true of picking the names of your friends' exes. They are unlikely to thank you if they have to say a name they loathe repeatedly. Just steer clear of any names you know will have problems for other people, paying particular attention to your partner and loved ones.

- **What if you can't agree?** This is probably the trickiest problem in the baby-naming process to solve. It's wise to research a number of names you and your partner are both interested in and make a point of discussing your reasons for liking or disliking them long before the baby is due to be born. The labour and delivery room is probably not the best time to argue as you'll both be tired, emotional, and at least one of you will be in pain. Avoid sticking to your guns on a name one of you really isn't happy with because it might lead to resentment down the line, with your baby caught in the middle. You could try compromising and picking two middle names so you both have a name in there you love, or you could each have five names you're allowed to 'veto' but no more. You could also try making contractions out of names you both like, such as Anna and Lisa (Annalisa) or James and Hayden (Jayden). Whichever way you go about it, it's important that you eventually agree on the name you are giving your baby, even if it means losing out on the one you've had your heart set on for a while.

Think to the future

66 Always end the name of your child with a vowel, so that when you yell the name will carry. 99

Bill Cosby

One important aspect of naming your child is thinking ahead to their future. Will the name you've chosen stand the test of time? Will names popular in 2013 remain popular in 2040? Will they be able to confidently enter a room and give a crucial business presentation with an awkward or unpronounceable name? Will they be able to hand their business card over to a potential client without that client looking bemused every time? Even on a smaller scale, can they survive the potential minefields of primary and secondary school with a name that could be easily shortened to something embarrassing?

While it seems a very long way off now, it is important to think about the impact your chosen name will have on your child's life, and how they will cope with that name as an adult. Introducing themselves as Professor Xavier to a group of university deans might raise a few smirks among knowing *X-Men* fans, as would any unusual or trendy 2013 name which has lost its shine by 2040. Would you want to try catching criminals as Police Officer Apple Blossom or have other politicians take you seriously with a name like MP Lil' Kim Scarlett? You don't want to give your child a name that they just cannot live with for the rest of their lives, so make your choice based on what's appropriate for a child as well as an adult. To make this easier you might want to choose a longer name that can be shortened or extended as your child desires.

Singer/actor Matt Willis dealt with this very problem in November 2011, when he announced the birth of his new baby son on Twitter. Willis wrote: 'I have a son and his name is Ace!' When a follower made a crack about the name, asking if the middle name would be 'Ventura', after the popular Jim Carrey character, Willis responded with: 'Nearly! Went for Billy so if he wants to be like a f**king banker or something he can use that instead!' Interestingly, All Saints' singer Natalie Appleton also named her son Ace Billy in 2004.

Names that should be banned

Anna Banana Baptista
Benson and Hedges (twins)
Ford Mustang
Hairy Berry
Kaos

Laxative Thomas
Masport and Mower (twins)
Midnight Chardonnay
Number 16 Bus Shelter
Spiral Cicada
Superman (changed from 4Real)
Violence

Stereotypes: true or false?

Will the name you choose actually affect your child's
life? Will names that seem clever make your child brainier?
Will names with positive meanings make your child into a
happier person? The answer is . . . possibly.

Some experts believe that parents who choose inspirational
names for their offspring (Destiny, Serenity, Unique) or
names of products they would like to own (Armani, Jaguar,
Mercedes) are projecting a future onto their child for them
to aspire to, and therefore help shape their child's life.
However, use this approach with caution: recent research
suggests girls who are given particularly 'girly' names –
think Tiana, Kayla, and Isabella – are much more likely
to misbehave when they reach school age, and it's even
more of a problem when there's more than one child in
the classroom with the same name. Poor Isabella. These
'feminine' girls were also far less likely to choose subjects at
school like maths and science, while their sisters with more
masculine names – such as Morgan, Alexis, and Ashley –
were encouraged to excel in these courses.

Inspirational names

Destiny	Joy
Happy	Peace
Heaven	Serenity
Hope	Unique
Innocence	Unity

Aspirational names

Armani	Ferrari
Aston	Jaguar
Bugatti	Mercedes
Chanel	Porsche
Dolce	Prada

One other thing to consider is how your child's name will be perceived by the outside world. Typically, judgements are passed on names before a person is met, such as at job interviews or in school. This does have the potential to hold back your child, although there is conflicting evidence to say that once someone is met in person, assumptions and stereotypes are wiped away. The strongest evidence at the moment suggests that self-esteem is linked to whether you like your name or not – so perhaps it doesn't really matter what name you pick, as long as your child likes it.

The latest research indicates that there are certain names more likely to initiate strong responses in people than others. A recent study analysed the number of stickers given to children as rewards for good behaviour. Children named Abigail and Jacob are more likely to be praised for being well behaved than children named Beth and Josh, and children who do not shorten their name or go by nicknames are more likely to be better behaved, too.

Top 10 names in New Zealand

Boys	Girls
1. Liam	1. Ruby
2. Joshua	2. Olivia
3. Oliver	3. Sophie
4. Lucas	4. Isabella
5. William	5. Charlotte
6. Noah	6. Grace
7. Samuel	7. Ella
8. James	8. Lily
9. Benjamin	9. Emily
10. Jack	10. Amelia

Last year, teachers across the country were asked to decide from a list of names which children were more likely to be badly behaved than others. Topping the 'naughty' charts were Callum, Connor, and Jack for boys, and Chelsea, Courtney, and Chardonnay for girls, while the names in the 'clever' category were Alexander, Adam, and Christopher for boys, and Elizabeth, Charlotte, and Emma for girls.

Teachers were also asked to pick names they felt were likely to be given to 'popular' children, and these included Jack, Daniel, Charlie, Emma, Charlotte, and Hannah – meaning little boys named Jack are naughty, but popular! Teachers in a different survey were asked to pick names they felt were particularly 'chavvy'. Chantelle, Jordan, Kylie, and Paige came out on top for the girls, and Connor, Dwayne, Liam, and Rhys were ranked first for the boys. Around the same time, it was discovered that teenagers named Katherine and Duncan (or a variation of the two, such as Kate) were up to eight times more likely to achieve high GCSE results than those named Wayne or Jermaine.

Names which mean 'clever'

Abner	Shanahan
Cassidy	Todd
Haley	Ulysses
Penelope	Washington
Portia	Wylie

Names which *sound* clever

Alastair	Gabriel
Charles	Harriet
Christian	Sophia
Elizabeth	Spencer
Frances	William

Children who are told they have inherited an ancestor's name or that of an influential character from history seem to be more driven and focused than children who are told disappointingly, 'we just liked the sound of it'. As a parent, it seems it's okay to pick an unusual name if you have the story or anecdotal evidence to back it up. Naming your child Atticus (after Atticus Finch from Harper Lee's *To Kill A Mockingbird*, known for being a strong and moral character) may therefore not be a bad idea . . . However, there is no actual scientific evidence to prove the power of names directly affects someone's life – it's all anecdotal.

Personality and character have a far greater influence than name alone and after a while, a name becomes just a name.

Quirky names

There are lots of disadvantages to having a quirky name, but there are plenty of advantages too. For one thing, your child's name will never be forgotten by other people, and if they do something influential with their life their name could become inspirational for other parents to name their

What not to call your child

In Pennsylvania a few years ago there was a case of a supermarket bakery refusing to ice the words 'Happy Birthday, Adolf Hitler' onto a three-year-old's birthday cake. The parents were able to eventually fulfil the order at another shop, but as a result of the publicity surrounding the event Social Services were called in to assess the child's home and Adolf, along with his siblings JoyceLynn Aryan Nation and Honszlynn Hinler Jeannie, were taken into care.

Controversial names adopted by real people

Adolf Hitler	Jezebel
Beelzebub	Lucifer
Desdemona	Mussolini
Hannibal Lecter	Stalin
Himmler	Voldemort

children. On the other hand, a quirky name often requires a quirky personality. If you don't think your genes could stand up to a name like Satchel or Kerensa, perhaps it's time to think of one a little more run-of-the-mill.

It's not true that babies are as influenced by their names as people believe. There is no scientific evidence to say that names dictate who we become, which means that you cannot give your child a perfect or imperfect name, whichever one you finally pick. However, a survey carried out recently by the National Centre for Social Research found that the more unusual the name, the less likely a candidate is to be called for a job interview after submitting a CV. Whether or not this fact would affect a child's development and future career is yet to be determined, but it is something to consider.

Disease names throughout history

Rubella Graves (born 1814)

Cholera Priest (born 1830)

Emma Royd (born 1850)

Fever Bender (born 1856)

Hysteria Johnson (born 1881)

Mumps Sykes (born 1891)

Kathryn E. Coli (born 1894)

Typhus Black (born 1897)

Leper Priest (born 1929)

There is also new research from baby website Bounty, which says that as many as one in five parents regrets their choice of baby name. Of the 3,000 parents interviewed, 20% said they no longer thought the unusual choice of spelling or pronunciation was appropriate. Around 8% said they were tired of people mispronouncing their child's name, and 10% thought the novelty of the original pick had worn off. They also said they would now pick a new name which had not occurred to them or been an option before.

While parents are often discouraged from picking wild and crazy names for their babies (think about little Blue Ivy, Beyonce's daughter, or Zuma Nesta Rock, Gwen Stefani's second son) there isn't actually any evidence to suggest that children are hindered in any way by them, unless they're really, really extreme.

Helen Fairey of Derby changed her name by deed poll to Christmas Fairy in 2010. She now works for a large hotel chain, ensuring guests have plenty of Christmas cheer every year.

Nicknames

66 Nicknames stick to people, and the most ridiculous are the most adhesive. 99

Thomas C. Haliburton

Nicknames are unavoidable. They can range from the common – Mike from Michael; Sam from Samantha – to the trendy, funny, or downright insulting. I've lost count of the number of Richards who refuse to be called 'Dick' or how many girls named Frances prefer 'Fran' to 'Fanny'.

The first time your child encounters a nickname will probably be before they're even born, or at least within the first few months. Many older siblings find new names hard to remember or pronounce and your baby could end up with a nickname before you know it. If your baby has an older sibling, try talking to them about their new brother or sister using the name you've chosen so you can discover how their imagination might choose to interpret it. If they're an older child you might even want to include them in the naming process from the start, if for no other reason than they mention a friend at school who gets teased for having an unfortunate nickname derived from the name you've chosen.

However, having said this, it is perfectly possible to choose a name that you know has an unfortunate nickname associated with it but for it to not bother you. If you don't encourage the use of nicknames when your child is young, the chances are one won't stick when they're older either. I, for example, don't tell anyone I meet as an adult that I was known as Nell for the better half of my childhood, so no one calls me that now. Another way to avoid embarrassing nicknames is to select one for your child that you actually like so that others don't even get a mention. Call your daughter Elizabeth by the names Liz, Lizzie, or Libby if you don't like Betty or Beth, and no one will even consider the alternatives.

You can pre-empt problem nicknames to some extent by saying the name you've chosen out loud and trying to find rhymes for it. This is a clever way to avoid playground chants and nursery rhyme-type insults, such as Andy Pandy or Looby Lou. It's a sad truth, though, that children will rhyme anything with anything else if they can, so while you might wish to take playground chants into account during your naming process, don't be too concerned about them. Most children are subjected to it at some point and emerge unscathed.

French law prohibits all names other than those on an approved list. However, in 2012 French courts allowed one couple to call their child 'Daemon' after a vampire character in the TV show *True Blood* – the first such deviation from the approved list in a decade.

Using family names

Some families have a strong tradition of using names for babies that come from the family tree. There are instances where naming your son Augustine VIII is simply not an option, it's a rule. Another way families do this is to give children the name of their parent of the same sex and add 'Junior' (Jr) to the end. This could potentially create a problem if that child then decides to carry on the tradition and name their child after themselves – after all, who wants to be known as Frederick Jr Jr? Admittedly this doesn't seem to happen very often in the UK but it is something to consider if this is one of your family's traditions.

There are pros and cons with using family names.

- **Pro:** Your child will feel part of a strong tradition, which will create a sense of security for them and help make them feel a complete member of the family.

- **Pro:** If you're having a problem selecting a name you and your partner both agree on, this is a very simple solution and will make your new child's family very happy.

- **Con:** You might not actually like the name that's being passed down. Naming your child the 12th Thumbelina in a row might not actually hold the same attraction for you as for the generation before.

- **Con:** Another drawback could be if the cultural associations with that name have changed in your lifetime and it is no longer appropriate.

Traditional names

Boys	Girls
Arthur	Ava
Charlie	Dorothy
Edward	Elizabeth
Fred	Grace
Harry	Louisa
Henry	Margaret
Joseph	Martha
Julian	Mary
Miles	Olivia
William	Rosemary

One way to navigate around choosing a family name is to compromise. You could use the name as a middle name, or refer to your baby by a nickname instead. You could also suggest using a name from the other partner's family: if the name comes from your side, try finding one you like from the other side. If their argument is for tradition then this is an astonishingly effective counter-argument.

Another possible solution is to use monikers – if your family is insisting your daughter be called Jade, maybe you could choose Giada instead. Or if your partner is determined the next child be called Michael after himself and it turns out to be a girl, choose Michaela in its place. In many Jewish families the tradition is to take the name of a dead relative and give it to a new baby. If this thought fills you with

Top 10 boys' names in 1914 and 1994

1914	**1994**
1. John	1. Thomas
2. William	2. James
3. George	3. Jack
4. Thomas	4. Daniel
5. James	5. Matthew
6. Arthur	6. Ryan
7. Frederick	7. Joshua
8. Albert	8. Luke
9. Charles	9. Samuel
10. Robert	10. Jordan

dread, you could opt for a possible solution a lot of families do, which is to use the first initial instead. If you're not keen on Solomon, pick Samuel; if you don't like Ruth, choose Rebecca.

Whatever you decide about using family names, just remember that this is *your* baby. Just as your parents got to decide what they named you, you get to decide this. If family and friends are disappointed, don't be alarmed. Once the baby is here all they will see is how much she has her grandmother's nose or his grandfather's ears, and the name will become far less important.

Top 10 girls' names in 1914 and 1994

1914	1994
1. Mary	1. Rebecca
2. Margaret	2. Lauren
3. Doris	3. Jessica
4. Dorothy	4. Charlotte
5. Kathleen	5. Hannah
6. Florence	6. Sophie
7. Elsie	7. Amy
8. Edith	8. Emily
9. Elizabeth	9. Laura
10. Winifred	10. Emma

Spellings and pronunciation

Once you've finally agreed upon a name, it's time to think about how you wish it to be spelt and pronounced. Some parents love experimenting with unusual variations of traditional names, while others prefer names to be instantly recognisable. The only advice here is to use caution in your experiments. There are many tales of parents seeing or hearing pretty names in the hospital during delivery and choosing them for their children, only to find out later they were medical terms and therefore completely inappropriate as names. Even spelling or pronouncing them differently won't be of much use once they're old enough to know the meaning behind them.

Medical terms used as names

The following list was provided by a practising midwife, who has vivid recollections of parents thinking they were naming their children something unique and original, only to be told the name they'd chosen was a medical term.

Chlamydia (pronounced cler-mid-EE-ya)

Eczema (pronounced ex-SEE-mah)

Female (pronounced fuh-MAH-lee)

Latrine (pronounced lah-TREE-nee)

Meconium (pronounced meh-COH-nee-um)

Syphilis (pronounced see-PHIL-iss)

Testicles (pronounced TESS-tee-clees)

Urine (pronounced yer-REE-nee)

Vagina (pronounced vaj-EE-nah)

Obviously the examples above are a little extreme, but the choices you make regarding spelling and pronunciation are really important. Try to avoid making a common name too long or too unusual in its spelling as this will be the first thing your child learns how to write. They will also be subjected to constant corrections during their lifetime, as other people misspell or mispronounce their name in ever more frustrating patterns. Make sure the name isn't too long that it won't fit on forms or name badges, as they'll simply stop using it and take on a nickname instead. Substituting the odd 'i' for a 'y' isn't too bad, but turning the name Jonathan into Jonnaythanne doesn't do anyone any favours.

Pronunciation matters: a Swedish couple were once banned from naming their child 'Brfxxccxxmnpccccllllmmnprxvclmnckssqlbb11116', which they claimed was pronounced 'Albin'.

Britain has seen an increase in 'text' language spellings

An Jaicub

Camron Jayk

Conna Lora

Ema Patryk

Esta Samiul

Flicity Summa

Helin Wilym

Middle names

The use of middle names is pretty standard practice these days. In fact, it has become fairly uncommon to name a child *without* a middle name, although the use of second and third names only become popular around the turn of the 20th century. Before then, giving a child a middle name in addition to a first and last was seen as a status symbol; it was only really used when a man married a higher-class woman and they wanted to keep the woman's maiden name as a reminder of that child's heritage. Once the fashion caught on it became very popular to give more than one middle name to children of status, but it's only been since the 1900s that it became standard for everyone.

Regardless of your status, a middle name can have just as much of an impact as a forename so your choice for your own baby should be made as carefully as their first name.

You may have already decided what middle name to give your child due to tradition or culture, in which case the following advice may be moot. In Spanish cultures, for example, middle names are often the mother's surname or other name to promote the matriarchal lineage. Similarly, parents who have not taken each other's surnames or are not married may choose to give their child one surname as a middle name and one as a last name so both parents are represented. Other traditions may use an old family name, passed down to each first-born son or daughter to encourage a sense of family pride and history. A decision about what middle name to pass on may have therefore already been made for you, even before your own birth.

Unique middle names are very much *en vogue* right now with celebrities. The Beckhams chose 'Seven' for their daughter's middle name, and there has been much discussion in the media as to why – could it be because Beckham's jersey number was seven, or that the little girl was born during the seventh hour, on the seventh day of the week, during the seventh month? Was it because the number seven is traditionally lucky? Who knows . . . Either way, the name Harper Seven has raised a few smirks as people point out the similarity to the expression 'Half past seven'!

The shortest baby names are only two letters long (Al, Ed, Jo, and Ty), but the longest could be any length imaginable. Popular 11 letter-long names include Bartholomew, Christopher, Constantine, and Maximillian.

If you are choosing a middle name there are some common trends for 2013 to help you narrow it down.

- **Opposite-length names.** It has become very popular to give a child either a long forename and short middle name, or a short forename and long middle name. If this idea attracts you, consider using syllables to give you an idea of length and combinations. Generally, if the forename has only one or two syllables (Owen, Steven, Yasmin, Zoe) then the middle name should have two, three, or even four syllables (Owen Jonathan, Steven Michael, Yasmin Samantha, Zoe Jessica). If the opposite is true and the forename is three or four syllables long (Anthony, Jennifer, Nicholas, Rosemary), the middle name may be better kept to only one or two syllables (Anthony Kevin, Jennifer Ruth, Nicholas John, Rosemary Dawn).

- **Names from the family tree.** Honouring your ancestors is another popular trend for 2013. Parents are frequently looking back to their own lineage for interesting, unusual or influential names.

Mariah Carey and Nick Cannon took two different approaches to middle names with their twins. They gave their baby boy Moroccan the middle name Scott – as it is not only Nick's middle name, but also his grandmother's maiden name – but decided not to give their baby girl Monroe a middle name, as Mariah doesn't have one either.

- **Unusual names.** Along with a wider variety of first names in recent years (Ruby, Amelia, and Mia have all climbed the Top 20 charts over the last few years), parents are choosing more unusual middle names too. This would make sense, as a child named Bronte or Keilyn probably needs a fairly uncommon middle name to balance it out. Alternatively, as middle names are far less frequently used, this is an opportunity for parents to have an unusual name included that they wouldn't perhaps use otherwise. If their child grows up not to like it they have the option of only using their initial, or simply dropping it from daily use altogether.

- **Common names.** As a last resort, if you find you are struggling to choose a middle name you could always pick a traditionally used one. For girls, Grace, Marie, May, and Rose have all been strikingly popular in 2012, and the same is true for Christopher, David, Jackson, and Thomas for boys.

It is becoming more and more common to give a parent's first name as a middle name to newborns.

Predicted popular middle names for 2013

Boys	Girls
Adam	Anne
Billy	Elise
Christopher	Elizabeth
David	Grace
Jackson	Leigh
Joseph	Marie
Lee	May
Michael	Nicole
Steven	Rose
Thomas	Ruth

As with first names, middle names can have hilarious consequences if not thought about carefully. It's worth writing down your favourite combinations and saying them out loud to make sure you're not making one of these mistakes . . .

Amusing middle name combinations

Brandy Ann Koch (brandy and coke)

Claire Annette Reed (clarinet reed)

Harry Armand Bach (hairy arm and back)

Justin Miles North (just ten miles north)

Laura Lynne Hardy (Laurel and Hardy)

Lisa May Boyle (Lisa may boil)

Mary Annette Woodin (marionette wooden)

Norma Leigh Lucid (normally lucid)

May Ann Naze (mayonnaise)

Sam Ann Fisher (salmon fisher)

Of course, you don't have to narrow down middle name choices to just one. It is becoming more and more common to have several middle names, particularly if parents like more than one or want to include a family name as well. Be careful not to have too many though, as this makes life very difficult when filling out official forms or enrolling your child in school. Most institutions only recognise one middle name, and some only recognise a middle initial.

Some famous examples of multiple middle names include British musician Brian Eno, whose full name is actually Brian Peter George St John le Baptiste de la Salle Eno, and Canadian actor Kiefer Sutherland, who has shortened his name considerably from Kiefer William Frederick Dempsey George Rufus Sutherland. Even the Royal Family likes to give many middle names: Prince Charles's full name is Charles Philip Arthur George Mountbatten-Windsor, and Prince William is William Arthur Philip Louis Mountbatten-Windsor.

Many people actually choose to go by their middle name instead of their forename, so it could be seen as a safety net if you're worried your child won't like their name. In fact, you probably know someone in your family or workplace who has always been known as Ed or Sam when their name is actually James Edward Jones or Felicity Samantha Taylor. It's also handy in this age of living online: if you search for John Smith or Jenny Brown you'll probably find hundreds and hundreds of results. However, if you search for John Ashok Smith or Jenny Marina Brown, there will probably be no more than one or two.

The Glastonbury teenager named Captain Fantastic Faster Than Superman Spiderman Batman Wolverine Hulk And The Flash Combined, changed his name from George Garratt in 2008. He claims to have the longest name in the world. If he does then he replaces Texan woman Rhoshandiatellyneshiaunneveshenk Koyaanisquatsiuth Williams, whose 57-letter length name pales in comparison to Captain's 81.

Celebrities who go by middle names

Antonio Banderas (José Antonio Dominguez Banderas)
Bob Marley (Nesta Robert Marley)
Dakota Fanning (Hannah Dakota Fanning)
Will Ferrell (John William Ferrell)
Kelsey Grammar (Allen Kelsey Grammar)

Ashton Kutcher (Christopher Ashton Kutcher)
Hugh Laurie (James Hugh Calum Laurie)
Evangeline Lilly (Nicole Evangeline Lilly)
Brad Pitt (William Bradley Pitt)
Brooke Shields (Christa Brooke Camille
    Shields)
Reese Witherspoon (Laura Jean Reese
    Witherspoon)

Initials

What surname will your baby have? Does its first letter
lend itself easily to amusing acronyms already, and would
choosing certain forenames only exacerbate the problem?

If your child will inherit a double-barrelled surname this
becomes a bigger consideration still, as there are more
amusing four letter words than there are three. My brother-
in-law was going to be called Andrew Steven Schmitt before
he was born, until his parents realised at the last minute
what his initials would spell . . .

It's worth taking the time to think about acronyms of initials
in the real world too, such as how names are displayed on
credit cards or imagining your child's name written out on
a form. Nobody should have to go through life known as S.
Lugg because their parents didn't think that far ahead.

Amusing initials

Earl E. Bird

Kay F. Cee

I. P. Freely

Al E. Gador

Angie O. Graham

S. Lugg

Warren T.

I.C. Blood

H. I. Vee

Gene E. Yuss

❝I call everyone 'darling' because I can't remember their names.❞

Zsazsa Gabor

Amusing acronyms of real people

Samuel Alan Spencer – SAS

Sally Theresa Donaghue – STD

Neil Christopher Parker – NCP (the car park)

James John Brookes – JJB (the sportswear shop)

Jake Clive Baxter – JCB

Patricia Mary Simpson – PMS

David Vernon Durante – DVD

Victoria Helen Smith – VHS

Jennifer Paige Garrett – JPG

George Barry Holmes – GBH

Across the UK, there are people whose initials spell out three letter words – from RAT and FAG to FAB or POP – and some are better than others, so do check!

Your surname

Tied to your child's potential new initials is their new surname. Whether they are receiving their name from their mother, father or a hyphenated combination of both, matching an appropriate first name to their surname is an important undertaking. Try to avoid forenames that might lead to unfortunate outcomes if they get combined with certain surnames, to prevent a lifetime of embarrassment for your baby. The best way to work out if this might happen is to write down all the names you like alongside your child's last name and have someone else read them out loud. This second pair of eyes and ears might just spot something you didn't.

Unfortunate first name/surname combinations

Anna Sasin

Barb Dwyer

Barry Cade

Ben Dover

Duane Pipe

Grace Land

Harry Rump

Hazel Nutt

Isabella Horn

Jenny Taylor

Justin Time

Mary Christmas

Oliver Sutton

Paige Turner

Russell Sprout

Stan Still

Teresa Green

The age of the internet has given parents a wonderful new weapon in their baby-naming arsenal: the search engine. Before you settle on anything final, try searching for any examples of the complete first, middle, and surname of your new baby. You may find out that your baby has an axe-murderer namesake – or, like one of my colleagues, the same name as a well-known porn star.

There is also the danger of your child being subjected to having a spoonerism made out of their name, where the first letters or syllables get swapped around to form new words. Named after the Reverend Dr William Archibald Spooner (1844–1930), a spoonerism can be created out of almost anything to make clever, amusing, or downright inappropriate phrases instead. An unfortunate and recent example of this would be Angelina Jolie and Brad Pitt's daughter Shiloh, whom they named Shiloh Jolie-Pitt to avoid the inevitable Shiloh Pitt spoonerism. Try to avoid making the same mistake!

Twitter has recently become a hot spot for spoonerisms, with celebrities such as Justin Bieber and Nick Jonas reportedly calling each other 'Bustin Jieber' and 'Jick Nonas'. After all, no one ever said spoonerisms have to make sense . . .

Celebrity spoonerisms

Mike Baker (bike maker)

Shirley Bassey (burly chassis)

Justin Bieber (bustin jieber)

Kelly Brook (belly crook)

Gordon Brown (broaden gown)

Nick Jonas (jick nonas)

Gene Kelly (keen jelly)

Jude Law (lewd jaw)

Sarah Palin (para sailing)

Shiloh Pitt (pile o' s***)

Wesley Snipes (snesley wipes)

Paul Walker (wall porker)

German law prohibits invented and androgynous names but the UK has some of the most liberal rules on naming a baby in the world, with only names which are deemed to be offensive making it onto the banned list.

4

Registering a baby's name

There are slightly different guidelines for registering births and names depending on where you live in the UK.

- In England, Wales and Northern Ireland a birth must be recorded within 42 days of delivery and if not done at the hospital it requires a visit to a register office.

- The birth certificate will be written in English if a child is born in England or Northern Ireland, and can be in both English and Welsh if they are born in Wales.

- If the birth is recorded at the hospital or registered in the same district, then birth certificates are usually issued straightaway, but if you end up going to a different office the certificate may be sent to you after a few days. This is important when applying for Child Benefits or registering your baby with a doctor as you will need a copy of the short birth certificate to apply.

> 66 Names are not always what they seem. The common Welsh name BZJXXLLWCP is pronounced Jackson. 99
>
> Mark Twain

- If the parents of a newborn are married, either parent can register a birth. However, if the parents are not married there are several ways to ensure both names are put on the birth certificate, including both parents being physically present at the registration or one parent submitting a declaration form in lieu of their presence. If neither parent can be present then someone who was present at the birth or someone who is now responsible for the child can also carry out the duty.

- After the registration, parents or those with parental responsibility also have the option of requesting a naming ceremony. These non-religious ceremonies are conducted by local authorities and can be a nice replacement for a baptism or Christening as adults outside of the family can be nominated to act in secular roles similar to godparents. A birth certificate is also needed for this event to take place.

- In Scotland births need to be registered within 21 days and can take place in any district. As well as either married parent being allowed to register the birth, relatives of those parents may also do the duty. The exception here is if the parents are not married. In this case the father may only register the birth if the mother is also present, a declaration form is submitted or a court agrees that he has parental responsibility just like any other adult. Parents of newborns in Scotland should take a card given to them at the hospital and a copy of their marriage certificate to the birth registration.

If you decide at a later stage you want to change details on the birth certificate there are procedures in place to help, although it is often a time-consuming process.

- It is worth remembering that if the father's details were not recorded on the original certificate or if the natural parents have married since the registration, a new birth certificate will have to be generated. Both changes require filling out an application form, available on the websites listed above.

- If you are unhappy with the forename you've chosen or it has been spelt incorrectly, you can change the birth record providing you have other documentation to prove this is the case. A passport or baptismal certificate

Useful websites for registering a birth

In **England and Wales:** www.direct.gov.uk
In **Northern Ireland:** www.groni.gov.uk
In **Scotland:** www.gro-scotland.gov.uk

is sufficient as they will show the correct spelling or commonly used forename and should be presented to the register office where the initial application was made.

- If you wish to change the surname of your baby it is only possible in two cases: either the spelling is incorrect or the details of the parents are being changed (such as the inclusion of the father or the parents now being married). Again, evidence and form submissions are needed to make any changes and a fee is usually incurred if a new certificate is required.

In 2011 Pope Benedict decreed all names should come from the Christian calendar. Italy promptly forbade one couple from naming their child 'Venerdi', meaning 'Friday', because it would open the boy up to ridicule and mockery. The parents threatened to name their next son 'Mercoledi', meaning 'Wednesday' in response.

Keep in mind how difficult it may be for you to change your child's birth certificate at a later stage if you are in any way unsure about the choice you're about to make. However, also remember that if something unexpected happens and you need to make the change, it is possible. There are stories of drunken fathers registering the birth of their child alone with a name not agreed upon by the mother, much to her horror. As Robert Eisenschmidt said, 'I have a friend, Bill Land, who named his daughter Alison Wanda Land. His wife changed the name on the birth certificate when she found out.' So it is possible, though obviously not preferred.

Popular names in South Africa

Boys	**Girls**
Abrahem	Abri
Baruti	Dikeledi
Dingane	Jacoline
Fenyang	Kagiso
Lefu	Limpho
Letsego	Mosa
Moswen	Nobanzi
Nku	Nomuula
Tau	Siphiwe
Uuka	Tale

5

Naming twins, triplets, and more

If you have discovered you are expecting multiples, congratulations! Naming multiples needn't be any different to naming a single child . . . unless you want it to be. You could stick to the same process everyone else does, by picking an individual name for each individual child. 'Octomom' Nadya Suleman chose eight different names for her octuplets, although they do all sound reasonably similar: Isaiah, Jeremiah, Jonah, Josiah, Maliah, McCai, Nariah, and Noah.

Another option is to go with a theme. Try anagrams or names in reverse, or give each child the same initials. You could do this even if you're not expecting multiples, like the Duggar family of Arkansas, USA, who have given each of their 19 children the initial 'J' – Joshua, Jana, John-David, Jill, Jessa, Jinger, Joseph, Josiah, Joy-Anna, Jedidiah, Jeremiah, Jason, James, Justin, Jackson, Johannah, Jennifer, Jordyn-Grace, and Josie. Their newest arrival was named Jubilee, although she sadly died in late 2011.

> The UK's biggest family title is currently held by the Shaws. Stacy and Tom Shaw have not chosen to follow a theme when naming their 13 children though: from oldest to youngest they are Shannon, Adam, Ryan, Kelsey, Franky, Leo, Laura, Keenan, Cody, Madison, Kaydn, Tyler, and Keavy.

Mariah Carey and Nick Cannon chose to use names starting with the same letter when naming their twins. Before announcing the names, Nick posted a clue to the names on Twitter, 'So we r bout 2 reveal the actual names and b4 we tell em 2 our friends etc. both begin w/M's!!!!' The couple then announced the arrival of Monroe and Moroccan Scott.

A palindrome name is a name that is spelt the same backwards and forwards, as with Bob, Elle, Eve, and Hannah.

Twin names with the same meaning

Bernard and Brian (strong)

Daphne and Laura (laurel)

Deborah and Melissa (bee)

Dorcas and Tabitha (gazelle)

Elijah and Joel (God)

Eve and Zoe (life)

Irene and Salome (peace)

Lucius and Uri (light)

Lucy and Helen (light)

Sarah and Almira (princess)

Popular twin names for 2013

Daniel and David

Ella and Emma

Gabriella and Isabella

Isaac and Isaiah

Jacob and Joshua

Madison and Morgan

Taylor and Tyler

Of course, when's all said and done you can just stick
to giving each child a name unique to them. For triplets,
quads, and more this is probably an easier choice than
twisting your head around three names with the same
meaning, or trying to create four anagrams you like for all of
your babies. Some parents do like to use a theme though,
such as going down the alphabet (think Alastair, Benjamin,

Christopher, and David), or doing what the famous acting Phoenix clan did and giving each child a name to do with nature: River, Rain, Joaquin (Leaf), Liberty, and Summer.

Names for triplets

Aidan, Diana, and Nadia (anagrams)
Amber, Jade, and Ruby (jewels)
Amy, May, and Mya (anagrams)
Ava, Eva, and Iva (similar)
Daisy, Lily, and Rose (flowers)
Jay, Raven, and Robin (birds)
Olive, Violet, and Sage (colours)
River, Rain, and Summer (nature)

Celebrity twin names of the past few years

Monroe and Moroccan Scott (Mariah Carey and Nick Cannon)
Darby and Sullivan (Patrick Dempsey and Jillian Fink)
Eddy and Nelson (Celine Dion and Rene Angelil)
Eden and Savannah (Marcia Cross and Tom Mahoney)
D'Lila Star and Jessie James (P Diddy and Kim Porter)
Hazel and Phinnaeus (Julia Roberts and Danny Moder)
Marion Loretta and Tabitha Hodge (Sarah Jessica Parker and Matthew Broderick)

Max and Bob (Charlie Sheen and Brooke
    Mueller)
Max and Emme (Jennifer Lopez and Marc Anthony)
Vivienne Marcheline and Knox Leon (Angelina Jolie
    and Brad Pitt)

Names, once they are in common use, quickly become mere sounds, their etymology being buried, like so many of the earth's marvel beneath the dust of habit.

Salman Rushdie

part two

Boys' Names

 Boys' names

Aaron

Hebrew, meaning 'mountain of strength'.

Abasi

Egyptian, meaning 'male'.

Abdiel

Biblical, meaning 'servant of God'.

Abdul

Arabic, meaning 'servant'. Often followed with a suffix indicating who Abdul is the servant of (e.g. Abdul-Basit, 'servant of the creator').

Abdullah

Arabic, meaning 'servant of God'.

Abe

Hebrew, from Abraham, meaning 'father'.

Abel

Hebrew, meaning 'breath' or 'breathing spirit'. Associated with the biblical son of Adam and Eve who was killed by his brother Cain.

Abelard

German, meaning 'resolute'.

Aberforth

Gaelic, meaning 'mouth of the river Forth'. Name of Dumbledore's brother in the Harry Potter books.

A

Abheek

Indian, meaning 'fearless'.

Abhishek

Indian, meaning 'bath for a deity' or 'anointing'.

Abner

Hebrew, meaning 'father of light'.

Absalom
(alt. Absalon)

Hebrew, meaning 'father/ leader of peace'.

Acacio

Greek, meaning 'thorny tree'. Now widely used in Spain.

Ace

English, meaning 'number one' or 'the best'.

Achilles

Greek, mythological hero of the Trojan war, whose heel was his only weak spot.

Achim

Hebrew, meaning 'God will establish' or Polish, meaning 'the Lord exalts'.

Ackerley

Old English, meaning 'oak meadow'. Often used as a surname.

Adalberto

Germanic/Spanish, meaning 'nobly bright'.

Adam

Hebrew, meaning 'man' or 'earth'. First man to walk the earth, accompanied by Eve.

Adão

Variant of Adam, meaning 'earth'.

Addison

Old English, meaning 'son of Adam'. Also used as a female name in the USA.

Ade

African, meaning 'peak' or 'pinnacle'.

A

Adelard

Teutonic, meaning 'brave' or 'noble'.

Adelbert

Old German form of Albert.

Aden

Gaelic, meaning 'fire'.

Adetokunbo

Yoruba, meaning 'the crown came from over the sea'.

Adin

Hebrew, meaning 'slender' or 'voluptuous'. Also Swahili, meaning 'ornamental'.

Aditya

Sanskrit, meaning 'belonging to the sun'.

Adlai

Hebrew, meaning 'God is just', or sometimes 'ornamental'.

Adler

Old German, meaning 'eagle'.

Adley

English, meaning 'son of Adam'.

Admon

Hebrew, variant of Adam meaning 'earth'. Also the name of a red peony.

Adolph
(alt. Adolf)

Old German, meaning 'noble majestic wolf'. Popularity of the name plummeted after the Second World War, for obvious reasons.

Adonis

Phoenician, meaning 'Lord'.

Movie inspirations

Austin *(Austin Powers)*
Don *(Singin' in the Rain)*
Edward (Twilight series)
Harry (Harry Potter series)
Jacob (Twilight series)
Jake *(Avatar)*
Korben *(The Fifth Element)*
Marty *(Back to the Future)*
Michael *(The Godfather)*
Renton *(Trainspotting)*
Wayne *(Wayne's World)*

A

Adrian

Latin, meaning 'from Hadria', a town in northern Italy.

Adriel

Hebrew, meaning 'of God's flock'.

Adyn

(alt. Adann, Ade, Aden)

Irish, meaning 'manly'.

Aeneas

Greek/Latin, meaning 'to praise'. Name of the hero who founded Rome in Virgil's *Aeneid*.

Aeson

Greek, father of Jason in Greek mythology.

Afonso

Portuguese, meaning 'eager noble warrior'.

Agamemnon

Greek, meaning 'leader of the assembly'. Figure in mythology, commanded the Greeks at the siege of Troy.

Agathon

Greek, meaning 'good' or 'superior'.

Agustin

Latin/Spanish, meaning 'venerated'.

Ahab

Hebrew, meaning 'father's brother'. Name of the obsessed captain in *Moby Dick*.

Ahijah

Hebrew, meaning 'brother of God' or 'friend of God'.

Ahmed

Arabic/Turkish, meaning 'worthy of praise'.

Aidan

(alt. Aiden)

Gaelic, meaning 'little fire'.

Aidric

Old English, meaning 'oaken'.

Airyck

Old Norse, from Eric, meaning 'eternal ruler'.

Ajani

African, meaning 'he fights for what he is'. Also Sanskrit, meaning 'of noble birth'.

Ajax

Greek, meaning 'mourner of the Earth'. Another Greek hero from the siege of Troy.

Ajay

Indian, meaning 'unconquerable'.

Ajit

Indian, meaning 'invincible'.

Akeem

Arabic, meaning 'wise or insightful'.

Akio

Japanese, meaning 'bright man'.

Akira

Japanese, meaning 'intelligent'.

Akiva

Hebrew, meaning 'to protect' or 'to shelter'.

Akon

American, made popular by the famous rapper charting in 2008/2009.

Aksel

Hebrew/Danish, meaning 'father of peace'.

Aladdin

Arabic, meaning 'servant of Allah'. From the medieval story in *Arabian Nights*.

Alan

(alt. Allan, Allen, Allyn, Alun)

Gaelic, meaning 'rock'.

Alaric

Old German, meaning 'noble regal ruler'.

Alastair

(alt. Alasdair, Allister)

Greek/Gaelic, meaning 'defending men'.

Alban

Latin, meaning 'from Alba'. Also the name of Saint Alban, the first British Christian martyr.

A

Alberic

Germanic, meaning 'Elfin king'.

Albert

Old German, meaning 'noble, bright, famous'.

Albin

Latin, meaning 'white'.

Albus

Latin, variant of Albin meaning 'white'. Also the Christian name of Albus Dumbledore, headmaster of Hogwarts School in the Harry Potter series.

Alcaeus

Greek, meaning 'strength'.

Alden

Old English, meaning 'old friend'.

Aldis

English, meaning 'from the old house'.

Aldo

Italian, meaning 'old' or 'elder'.

Aldric

English, meaning 'old King'.

Alec

(alt. Alek)

English, meaning 'defending men'.

Aled

Welsh, meaning 'child' or 'offspring'.

Aleph

Hebrew, meaning 'first letter of the alphabet', or 'leader'.

Aleron

(alt. Aileron, Alerun, Ailerun, Alejandro)

Latin, meaning 'child with wings'.

Alessio

Italian, meaning 'defender'.

Alexander

(alt. Alexandro, Alessandro, Alejandro)

Greek, meaning 'defending men'.

Alexei

Russian, meaning 'defender'.

Alfonso

Germanic/Spanish, meaning 'noble and prompt, ready to struggle'.

Alford
Old English, meaning 'old river/ford'.

Alfred
(alt. Alf, Alfi)
English, meaning 'elf' or 'magical counsel'.

Algernon
French, meaning 'with a moustache'.

Ali
(alt. Allie)
Arabic, meaning 'noble, sublime'.

Alois
German, meaning 'famous warrior'.

Alok
Indian, meaning 'cry of triumph'.

Alon
Jewish, meaning 'oak tree'.

Alonso
(alt. Alonzo)
Germanic, meaning 'noble and ready'.

Aloysius
Italian saint's name, meaning 'fame and war'.

Alpha
First letter of the Greek alphabet.

Alphaeus
Hebrew, meaning 'changing'.

Alpin
Gaelic, meaning 'related to the Alps'.

Altair
Arabic, meaning 'flying' or 'bird'.

Alter
Yiddish, meaning 'old man'.

Alton
Old English, meaning 'old town'.

Alva
Latin, meaning 'white'.

A

Alvie

German, meaning 'army of elves'.

Alvin

English, meaning 'friend of elves'.

Alwyn

Welsh, meaning 'wise friend'. May also come from the River Alwen in Wales.

Amachi

African, meaning 'who knows what God has brought us through this child'.

Amadeus

Latin, meaning 'God's love'.

Amadi

African, meaning 'appeared destined to die at birth'.

Amado

Spanish, meaning 'God's love'.

Amador

Spanish, meaning 'one who loves'.

Amari

Hebrew, meaning 'given by God'.

Amarion

Arabic, meaning 'populous, flushing'.

Amasa

Hebrew, meaning 'burden'.

Ambrose

Greek, meaning 'undying, immortal'.

Americo

Germanic, meaning 'ever powerful in battle'.

Amias

Latin, meaning 'loved'.

Amil

African, meaning 'effective'.

Amir

Hebrew, meaning 'prince' or 'treetop'.

Amit

Hindu, meaning 'friend'.

Ammon

Egyptian, meaning 'the hidden one'.

Amory

German/English, meaning 'work' and 'power'.

Amos

Hebrew, meaning 'encumbered' or 'burdened'.

Anacletus

Latin, meaning 'called back' or 'invoked'.

Anakin

American, meaning 'warrior'. Made famous by Anakin Skywalker in the Star Wars films.

Ananias

Greek/Italian, meaning 'answered by the Lord'.

Anastasius

Latin, meaning 'resurrection'.

Anat

Jewish, meaning 'water spring'.

Anatole

Greek, meaning 'cynical but without malice'.

Anders

Greek, meaning 'lion man'.

Anderson

English, meaning 'male'.

Andrew
(alt. Andreas)

Greek, meaning 'man' or 'warrior'.

Androcles

Greek, meaning 'glory of a warrior'.

Angel

Greek, meaning 'messenger'.

Angus

Scottish, meaning 'one choice'.

Anil

Sanskrit, meaning 'air' or 'wind'.

Anselm

German, meaning 'helmet of God'.

A

Anson
English, meaning 'son of Agnes'.

Anthony
English, from the old Roman family name.

Antipas
Israeli, meaning 'for all or against all'.

Antwan
Old English, meaning 'flower'.

Apollo
Greek, meaning 'to destroy'. Greek god of the sun.

Apostolos
Greek, meaning 'apostle'.

Ara
Armenian. Ara was a legendary king.

Aragorn
Literary, used by Tolkien in *The Lord of the Rings* trilogy.

Aram
Hebrew, meaning 'Royal Highness'.

Aramis
Latin, meaning 'swordsman'.

Arcadio
Greek/Spanish, from a place in ancient Greece. The word 'Arcadia' (meaning paradise) comes from this.

Archibald
(alt. Archie)
Old German, meaning 'genuine, bold, brave'.

Ardell
Latin, meaning 'eager, burning with enthusiasm'.

Arden
Celtic, meaning 'high'.

Ares
Greek, meaning 'ruin'. Son of Zeus and Greek god of war.

A

Ari

Hebrew, meaning 'lion' or 'eagle'.

Arias

Germanic, meaning 'lion'.

Aric

English, meaning 'merciful ruler'.

Ariel

Hebrew, meaning 'lion of God'. One of the archangels, the angel of healing and new beginnings.

Arild

Old Norse, meaning 'battle commander'.

Aris

Greek, meaning 'best figure'.

Ariston

Greek, meaning 'the best'.

Aristotle

Greek, meaning 'best'. Also a famous philosopher.

Arjun

Sanskrit, meaning 'white'.

Arkady

Greek, region of central Greece.

Arlan

Gaelic, meaning 'pledge' or 'oath'.

Arlie

Old English place name, meaning 'eagle wood'.

Arlis

Hebrew, meaning 'pledge'.

Arlo

Spanish, meaning 'barberry tree'.

Armand

Old German, meaning 'soldier'.

Armani

Same origin as Armand meaning 'soldier'. Nowadays closely associated with the Italian designer.

A

Arnaldo

Spanish, meaning 'eagle power'.

Arnav

Indian, meaning 'the sea'.

Arnold

Old German, meaning 'eagle ruler'.

Arrow

English, from the common word denoting weaponry.

Art

Irish, name of a warrior in Irish mythology, Art Oenfer (Art the Lonely).

Arthur

(alt. Artie, Artis)

Celtic, probably from 'artos', meaning 'bear'. Made famous by the tales of King Arthur and the Knights of the Round Table.

Arvel

From the Welsh 'Arwel', meaning 'wept over'.

Arvid

English, meaning 'eagle in the woods'.

Arvind

Indian, meaning 'red lotus'.

Arvo

Finnish, meaning 'value' or 'worth'.

Arwen

Welsh, meaning 'fair' or 'fine'.

Asa

Hebrew, meaning 'doctor' or 'healer'.

Asante

African, meaning 'thank you'.

Asher

Hebrew, meaning 'fortunate' or 'lucky'.

Ashley

Old English, meaning 'ash meadow'.

Ashok

Sanskrit, meaning 'not causing sorrow'.

A

Ashton

English, meaning 'settlement in the ash-tree grove'.

Aslan

Turkish, meaning 'lion'. Strongly associated with the lion from C. S. Lewis' *The Lion, the Witch, and the Wardrobe*.

Asriel

Hebrew, meaning 'help of God'.

Astrophel

Latin, meaning 'star lover'.

Athanasios

Greek, meaning 'eternal life'.

Atílio

Portuguese, meaning 'father'.

Atlas

Greek, meaning 'to carry'. In Greek mythology Atlas was a Titan forced to carry the weight of the heavens.

Atlee

Hebrew, meaning 'God is just'.

Atticus

Latin, meaning 'from Athens'.

Auberon

Old German, meaning 'royal bear'.

Aubrey

Old German, meaning 'power'.

Auden

Old English, meaning 'old friend'.

Audie

Old English, meaning 'noble strength'.

Long names

Alexander
Bartholomew
Christopher
Demetrius
Giovanni
Montgomery
Obadiah
Roberto
Salvatore
Zachariah

A

Augustas
(alt. Augustus)
Latin, meaning 'venerated'.

Aurelien
French, meaning 'golden'.

Austin
Latin, meaning 'venerated'.
Also a city in the state of Texas
in the USA.

Avi
Hebrew, meaning 'father of a
multitude of nations'.

Avery
(alt. Avrie, Averey, Averie)
English, meaning 'wise ruler'.

Awnan
Irish, meaning 'little Adam'.

Axel
Hebrew, meaning 'father is
peace'. Made famous by Guns
'n' Roses front man Axl Rose.

Ayers
(alt. Ayer, Aires, Aire)
English, meaning 'heir to a
fortune'.

Azarel
Hebrew, meaning 'helped by
God'.

Azaryah
Hebrew, meaning 'helped by
God'.

Azriel
Hebrew, meaning 'God is my
help'.

Azuko
African, meaning 'past glory'.

Boys' names

Baden

German, meaning 'battle'.

Bailey

English, meaning 'bailiff'.

Baird

Scottish, meaning 'poet' or 'one who sings ballads'.

Bakari

Swahili, meaning 'hope' or 'promise'.

Baker

English, from the word 'baker'.

Baldwin

Old French, meaning 'bold, brave friend'.

Balin

Old English. Balin was one of the Knights of the Round Table.

Balthazar

Babylonian, meaning 'protect the King'.

Balvinder

Hindu, meaning 'merciful, compassionate'.

Bannon

Irish, meaning 'descendant of O'Banain'. Also a river in Wales.

Barack

African, meaning 'blessed'. Made popular by US President Barack Obama.

B

Barclay

Old English, meaning 'birch tree meadow'. Also Persian, meaning 'messenger'.

Barker

Old English, meaning 'shepherd'.

Barnaby
(alt. Barney)

Greek, meaning 'son of consolation'.

Barnard

English, meaning 'strong as a bear'.

Baron

Old English, meaning 'young warrior'.

Barrett

English, meaning 'strong as a bear'.

Barron

Old German, meaning 'old clearing'.

Barry

Irish Gaelic, meaning 'fair haired'. Also a town in South Wales, made popular by the BBC TV series *Gavin and Stacey*.

Bart

Hebrew, from Bartholomew, meaning 'son of the farmer'. Made popular by the famous American TV character Bart Simpson.

Barton

Old English, meaning 'barley settlement'.

Baruch

Hebrew, meaning 'blessed'.

Barzillai

Hebrew, meaning 'my iron'.

Bashir

Arabic, meaning 'well-educated' and 'wise'.

Basil

Greek, meaning 'royal, kingly'.

B

Basim
Arabic, meaning 'smile'.

Bastien
Greek, meaning 'revered'.

Baxter
Old English, meaning 'baker'.

Bayard
French, meaning 'auburn haired'.

Bayre
American, meaning 'beautiful'.

Bayo
Nigerian, meaning 'to find joy'.

Baz
Irish Gaelic, meaning 'fair-haired'.

Beau
French, meaning 'handsome'.

Beck
Old Norse, meaning 'stream'.

Beckett
Old English, meaning 'beehive' or 'bee cottage'. Associated with the Irish writer Samuel Beckett.

Beckham
English, meaning 'homestead by the stream'. Made famous by David and Victoria Beckham.

Béla
Hungarian, meaning 'within'.

Belarius
Shakespearean, meaning 'a banished lord'.

Benedict
Latin, meaning 'blessed'.

Biblical names

Abel
Cain
Eli
Joseph
Luke
Mark
Moses
Paul
Peter
Solomon

B

Benicio

Spanish, meaning 'benevolent'.

Benjamin
(alt. Ben)

Hebrew, meaning 'son of the south'.

Bennett

French/Latin vernacular form of Benedict, meaning 'blessed'.

Benoit

French form of Benedict, meaning 'blessed'.

Benson

English, meaning 'son of Ben'. Also linked to the village of Benson in Oxfordshire.

Bentley

Old English, meaning 'bent grass meadow'.

Benton

Old English, meaning 'town in the bent grass'.

Beriah

Hebrew, meaning 'in fellowship' or 'in envy'.

Bernard
(alt. Bernie)

Germanic, meaning 'strong, brave bear'.

Berry

Old English, meaning 'berry'.

Bert
(alt. Bertram/Bertrand)

Old English, meaning 'illustrious'.

Berton

Old English, meaning 'bright settlement'.

Bevan

Welsh, meaning 'son of Evan'.

Bilal

Arabic, meaning 'wetting, refreshing'.

Bill
(alt. Billy)

English, from William, meaning 'determined' or 'resolute'.

Birch

Old English, meaning 'bright' or 'shining'.

B

Birger
Norwegian, meaning 'rescue'.

Bishop
Old English, meaning 'bishop'.

Bjorn
Old Norse, meaning 'bear'.

Bladen
Hebrew, meaning 'hero'.

Blaine
Irish Gaelic, meaning 'yellow'.

Blair
English, meaning 'plain'.

Blaise
French, meaning 'lisp' or 'stutter'.

Blake
Old English, meaning 'dark, black'.

Blas
(alt. Blaze)
German, meaning 'firebrand'.

Bo
Scandinavian, short form of Robert, meaning 'bright fame'.

Boaz
Hebrew, meaning 'swiftness' or 'strength'.

Bob
(alt. Bobby)
Old German, from Robert meaning 'bright fame'.

Boden
(alt. Bodie)
Scandinavian, meaning 'shelter'.

Bogumil
Slavic, meaning 'God's favour'.

Bolivar
Spanish, meaning 'the bank of the river'.

Bond
Old English, meaning 'peasant farmer'.

Boris
Slavic, meaning 'battle glory'.

B

Saints' names

Aidan
Bernard
Francis
Gabriel
Kieran
Nicholas
Patrick
Stephen
Thomas
Vincent

Bosten

English, meaning 'town by the woods'.

Botolf

English, meaning 'wolf'.

Bowen

Welsh, meaning 'son of Owen'.

Boyd

Scottish Gaelic, meaning 'yellow'.

Brad

(alt. Bradley)

Old English, meaning 'broad' or 'wide'.

Brady

Irish, meaning 'large-chested'.

Bradyn

Gaelic, meaning 'descendant of Bradan'.

Bram

Gaelic, meaning 'raven'.

Brandon

Old English, meaning 'gorse'.

Brandt

Old English, meaning 'beacon'.

Brannon

Gaelic, meaning 'raven'.

Branson

English, meaning 'son of Brand'.

Brant

Old English, meaning 'hill'.

Braulio

Greek, meaning 'shining'.

Brendan

Gaelic, meaning 'prince'.

B

Brennan

Gaelic, meaning 'teardrop'.

Brenton

English, from Brent, meaning 'hill'.

Brett

English, meaning 'a brewer'.

Brewster

(alt. Brew, Brewer)

English, meaning 'a brewer'.

Brian

Gaelic, meaning 'high' or 'noble'.

Brice

Latin, meaning 'speckled'.

Brier

French, meaning 'heather'.

Brock

Old English, meaning 'badger'.

Broderick

English, meaning 'ruler'.

Brody

Gaelic, meaning both 'ditch' and 'brother'.

Brogan

Irish, meaning 'sturdy shoe'.

Bronwyn

Welsh, meaning 'white breasted'.

Brook

English, meaning 'stream'.

Bruce

Scottish, meaning 'high' or 'noble'.

Bruno

Germanic, meaning 'brown'.

Brutus

Latin, meaning 'dim-wit'. The name of Julius Caesar's assassin.

Bryant

English variant of Brian, meaning 'high' or 'noble'.

B

Bryce
Scottish, meaning 'of Britain'.

Brycen
Scottish, meaning 'son of Bryce'.

Bryden
Irish, meaning 'strong one'.

Bryson
Welsh, meaning 'descendant of Brice'.

Bubba
American, meaning 'boy'.

Buck
American, meaning 'goat' or 'deer'.

Bud
(alt. Buddy)
American, meaning 'friend'.

Burdett
Middle English, meaning 'bird'.

Burgess
(alt. Burges, Burgiss, Berje)
English, meaning 'business'.

Burke
French, meaning 'fortified settlement'.

Burl
French, meaning 'knotty wood'.

Buzz
American, shortened form of Busby, meaning 'village in the thicket'. Associated with the astronaut Buzz Aldrin.

Byron
Old English, meaning 'barn'. Made famous by the poet Lord Byron.

Sci-fi names

Anakin
Balin
Chike
Dante
Faizah
Fola
Hahzara
Kanene
Kibo
Shatea
Umi

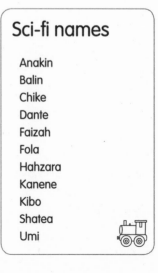

Boys' names

Cabot
Old English, meaning 'to sail'.

Cadby
(alt. Cadbey, Cadbee, Cadbie)
English, meaning 'soldier's colony'.

Cade
(alt. Caden)
English, meaning 'round, lumpy'.

Cadence
Latin, meaning 'with rhythm'.

Cadogan
Welsh, meaning 'battle glory and honour'.

Caedmon
Celtic, meaning 'wise warrior'.

Caelan
Gaelic, meaning 'slender'.

Caerwyn
(alt. Carwyn, Gerwyn)
Welsh, meaning 'white fort' or 'settlement'.

Caesar
Latin, meaning 'head of hair'. Made famous by the first Roman emperor Julius Caesar.

Caetano
Portuguese, meaning 'from Gaeta, Italy'.

Cagney
Irish, meaning 'successor of the advocate'.

C

Caiden
Arabic, meaning 'companion'.

Caillou
French, meaning 'pebble'.

Cain
Hebrew, meaning 'full of beauty'.

Cainan
Hebrew, meaning 'possessor' or 'purchaser'.

Cairo
Egyptian city.

Cal
Short form of names beginning Cal-.

Calder
Scottish, meaning 'rough waters'.

Caleb
Hebrew, meaning 'dog'.

Calen
From Caleb, meaning 'dog'.

Calhoun
Irish, meaning 'slight woods'.

Calix
Greek, meaning 'very handsome'.

Callahan
Irish, meaning 'contention' or 'strife'.

Callum
Gaelic, meaning 'dove'.

Calvin
French, meaning 'little bald one'.

Camden
Gaelic, meaning 'winding valley'. Also an area of north London.

Cameron
Scottish Gaelic, meaning 'crooked nose'.

Camillo
Latin, meaning 'free born' or 'noble'.

Campbell
Scottish Gaelic, meaning 'crooked mouth'.

C

Canaan

Hebrew, meaning 'to be humbled'.

Candido

Latin, meaning 'candid' or 'honest'.

Cannon

French, meaning 'of the church'.

Canton

French, meaning 'dweller of corner'. Also name given to areas of Switzerland.

Canute

(alt. Cnut, Cnute)
Scandinavian, meaning 'knot'. Name of the King of England in the 11th century.

Cappy

Italian, meaning 'lucky'.

Carden

Old English, meaning 'wool carder'.

Carey

Gaelic, meaning 'love'.

Carl

Old Norse, meaning 'free man'.

Carlo

Italian form of Carl, meaning 'free man'.

Carlos

Spanish form of Carl, meaning 'free man'.

Carlton

Old English, meaning 'free peasant settlement'.

Carmelo

Latin, meaning 'garden' or 'orchard'.

Carmen

Latin/Spanish, meaning 'song'.

Carmine

Latin, meaning 'song'.

Carnell

English, meaning 'defender of the castle'.

Carson

(alt. Carsten)
Scottish, meaning 'marsh-dwellers'.

Carter

Old English, meaning 'transporter of goods'.

C

Cary

Old Celtic river name. Also means 'love'.

Case

(alt. Casey)

Irish Gaelic, meaning 'alert' or 'watchful'.

Cash

Latin, shortened form of Cassius, meaning 'vain'.

Casimer

Slavic, meaning 'famous destroyer of peace'.

Cason

Latin, from Cassius, meaning 'empty' or 'hollow'.

Casper

Persian, meaning 'treasurer'.

Caspian

English, meaning 'of the Caspy people'. From the Caspian Sea.

Cassidy

Gaelic, meaning 'curly haired'.

Cassius

(alt. Cassio)

Latin, meaning 'empty, hollow'.

Cathal

Celtic, meaning 'battle rule'.

Cato

Latin, meaning 'all-knowing'.

TV personality names

Anthony (McPartlin)
Bruce (Forsyth)
Chris (Evans, Moyles)
Declan (Donnelly)
Dermot (O'Leary)
Graham (Norton)
Louis (Walsh)
Michael (McIntyre)
Phillip (Schofield)
Piers (Morgan)
Simon (Cowell)
Vernon (Kay)

Cecil

Latin, meaning 'blind'.

Cedar

English, from the name of an evergreen tree.

Cedric

Welsh, meaning 'spectacular bounty'.

Celestino

Spanish/Italian, meaning 'heavenly'.

Celesto
(alt. Celindo)

Latin, meaning 'heaven sent'.

Chad
(alt. Chadrick)

Old English, meaning 'warlike, warrior'.

Chaim

Hebrew, meaning 'life'.

Champion

English, from the word 'champion', meaning 'warrior'.

Chance

English, from the word 'chance' meaning 'good fortune'.

Chandler

Old English, meaning 'candle maker and seller'.

Charles
(alt. Charlie)

Old German, meaning 'free man'.

Chaska

Native American name usually given to first son.

Che

Spanish, shortened form of José. Made famous by Che Guevara.

Chesley

Old English, meaning 'camp on the meadow'.

Chester

Latin, meaning 'camp of soldiers'.

Chilton
(alt. Chillron, Chilly, Chilt)

English, meaning 'tranquil'.

C

Chima
Old English, meaning 'hilly land'.

Christian
English, from the word 'Christian'.

Christophe
French variant of Christopher, meaning 'bearing Christ inside'.

Christopher
Greek, meaning 'bearing Christ inside'.

Cian
Irish, meaning 'ancient'.

Ciaran
Irish, meaning 'black'.

Cicero
Latin, meaning 'chickpea'. Famous Roman philosopher and orator.

Cimarron
City in western Kansas.

Ciprian
Latin, meaning 'from Cyprus'.

Ciro
Spanish, meaning 'sun'.

Clancy
Old Irish, meaning 'red warrior'.

Clarence
Latin, meaning 'one who lives near the river Clare'.

Clark
Latin, meaning 'clerk'.

Claude
(alt. Claudie, Claudio, Claudius)
Latin, meaning 'lame'.

Claus
Variant of Nicholas, meaning 'people of victory'.

Clay
English, from the word 'clay'.

Clement
(alt. Clem)
Latin, meaning 'merciful'.

Cleo
Greek, meaning 'glory'.

C

Cletus
Greek, meaning 'illustrious'.

Cliff
(alt. Clifford, Clifton)
English, from the word 'cliff'.

Clint
(alt. Clinton)
Old English, meaning 'fenced settlement'.

Clive
Old English, meaning 'cliff' or 'slope'.

Clyde
Scottish, from the river in Glasgow.

Coby
(alt. Cody, Colby)
Irish, meaning 'son of Oda'.

Colden
Old English, meaning 'dark valley'.

Cole
Old French, meaning 'coal black'.

Coley
Old English, meaning 'coal black'.

Colin
Gaelic, meaning 'young creature'.

Colson
Old English, meaning 'coal black'.

Colton
English, meaning 'swarthy'.

Columbus
Latin, meaning 'dove'.

Colwyn
Welsh, from the river in Wales.

Conan
Gaelic, meaning 'wolf'.

Conley
Gaelic, meaning 'sensible'.

Connell
(alt. Connolly)
Irish, meaning 'high' or 'mighty'.

Connor
(alt. Conrad, Conroy)
Irish, meaning 'lover of hounds'.

Constant
(alt. Constantine)
English, from the word 'constant'.

Cooper
Old English, meaning 'barrel maker'.

Corban
Hebrew, meaning 'dedicated and belonging to God'.

Uncommon three-syllable names

Alastair
Barnaby
Dominic
Dorian
Elijah
Elliot
Lancelot
Roberto
Theodore

Corbett
(alt. Corbin, Corby)
Norman French, meaning 'young crow'.

Cordell
Old English, meaning 'cord maker'.

Corey
(alt. Cory)
Gaelic, meaning 'hill hollow'.

Corin
Latin, meaning 'spear'.

Corliss
(alt. Corlis, Corlyss, Corlys)
English, meaning 'benevolent'.

Cormac
Gaelic, meaning 'impure son'.

Cornelius
(alt. Cornell)
Latin, meaning 'horn'.

Cortez
Spanish, meaning 'courteous'.

Corwin

Old English, meaning 'heart's friend' or 'companion'.

Cosimo
(alt. Cosme, Cosmo)

Italian, meaning 'order' or 'beauty'.

Coty

French, meaning 'riverbank'.

Coulter

English, meaning 'young horse'.

Courtney

Old English, meaning 'domain of Curtis'.

Covey

English, meaning 'flock of birds'.

Cowan

Gaelic, meaning 'hollow in the hill'.

Craig

Welsh, meaning 'rock'.

Crispin

Latin, meaning 'curly haired'.

Croix

French, meaning 'cross'.

Cruz

Spanish, meaning 'cross'. Made famous by David and Victoria Beckham's son.

Cullen

Gaelic, meaning 'handsome'.

Curran

Gaelic, meaning 'dagger' or 'hero'.

Curtis
(alt. Curt)

Old French, meaning 'courteous'.

Cutler

Old English, meaning 'knife maker'.

Cyprian

English, meaning 'from Cyprus'.

Cyril

Greek, meaning 'master' or 'Lord'.

Cyrus

Persian, meaning 'Lord'.

Prime Ministers' names

Anthony (Eden, Blair)
Arthur (Wellesley, Balfour, Chamberlain)
David (Cameron)
Charles (Wentworth, Grey)
George (Grenville, Canning, Gordon)
Gordon (Brown)
Harold (Macmillan, Wilson)
Henry (Pelham, Fitzroy, Addington, Temple,
   Campbell-Bannerman, Asquith)
James (Balfour, MacDonald, Wilson)
John (Stuart, Russell, Major)
Robert (Walpole, Jenkinson, Peel, Gascoyne-Cecil)
Spencer (Crompton, Perceval)
William (Cavendish, Pitt (Elder and Younger),
   Wyndham, Lamb, Gladstone)

Boys' names

Dabeel
(alt. Dabee, Dabie, Daby)
Indian, meaning 'warrior'.

Dafydd
Welsh, meaning 'beloved'.
Made famous by the character
in the BBC TV series *Little
Britain*.

Daichi
Japanese, meaning 'great
wisdom'.

Daire
(alt. Daer, Daere, Dair)
Irish, meaning 'wealthy'.

Daisuke
Japanese, meaning
'lionhearted'.

Dakari
African, meaning 'happy'.

Dale
Old English, meaning 'valley'.

Dallin
English, meaning 'dweller in the
valley'.

Dalton
English, meaning 'town in the
valley'.

Daly
Gaelic, meaning 'assembly'.

Damarion
Greek, meaning 'gentle'.

D

Damian
(alt. Damon)
Greek, meaning 'to tame, subdue'.

Dane
Old English, meaning 'from Denmark'.

Daniel
(alt. Dan, Danny)
Hebrew, meaning 'God is my judge'.

Dante
Latin, meaning 'lasting'. Associated with the Italian 13th century poet Dante Alighieri author of *The Divine Comdey*.

Darby
Irish, meaning 'without envy'.

Darcy
Gaelic, meaning 'dark'. Associated with Jane Austen's Mr Darcy, and the parody of this character in *Bridget Jones' Diary*.

Dario
(alt. Darius)
Greek, meaning 'kingly'.

Darnell
Old English, meaning 'the hidden spot'.

Darragh
Irish, meaning 'dark oak'.

Darrell
(alt. Daryl)
Old English, meaning 'open'.

Darren
(alt. Darrian)
Gaelic, meaning 'great'.

Darrick
Old German, meaning 'power of the tribe'.

Darshan
Hindi, meaning 'vision'.

Darwin
Old English, meaning 'dear friend'. Often associated with the naturalist Charles Darwin.

Dash
(alt. Dashawn)
American, meaning 'enlightened one'.

D

Dashiell

French, meaning 'page boy'.

Dason

Native American, meaning 'chief'.

David

(alt. Dave, Davey, Davie, Davin)

Hebrew, meaning 'beloved'.

Davis

Old English, meaning 'son of David'.

Dawson

Old English, meaning 'son of David'.

Dax

(alt. Daxton)

French, once a town in south-western France. Now associated with the *Star Trek* character.

Dayal

Indian, meaning 'kind'.

Dayton

Old English, meaning 'David's place'.

Dean

Old English, meaning 'valley'.

Declan

Irish, meaning 'full of goodness'.

Dedric

Old English, meaning 'gifted ruler'.

Deepak

(alt. Deepan)

Indian, meaning 'illumination'.

Del

(alt. Delano, Delbert, Dell)

Old English, meaning 'bright shining one'.

Delaney

Irish, meaning 'dark challenge'.

Demetrius

Greek, meaning 'harvest lover'.

Dempsey

Irish, meaning 'proud'.

Denham

(alt. Denholm)

Old English, meaning 'valley settlement'.

D

Old name, new fashion?

Bertrand
Dexter
Felix
Hector
Jefferson
Norris
Pierce
Reginald
Ulysses
Winston

Dennis
(alt. Denny, Denton)

English, meaning 'follower of Dionysius'.

Denzil
(alt. Denzel)

English, meaning 'fort'. Also a town in Cornwall.

Deon

Greek, meaning 'of Zeus'.

Derek

English, meaning 'power of the tribe'.

Dermot

Irish, meaning 'free man'.

Desmond

Irish, meaning 'from south Munster'.

Destin

French, meaning 'destiny'.

Devyn

Irish, meaning 'poet'.

Dewey

Welsh, from Dewi (David).

Dexter
(alt. Dex)

Latin, meaning 'right-handed'.

Diallo
(alt. Dialo)

African, meaning 'bold'.

Dick
(alt. Dickie, Dickon)

From Richard, meaning 'powerful leader'.

Didier

French, meaning 'much desired'.

D

Diego

Spanish, meaning 'supplanter'.

Dietrich

Old German, meaning 'power of the tribe'.

Diggory

English, meaning 'dyke'.

Dilbert

English, meaning 'day-bright'.

Dimitri

(alt. Dimitrios, Dimitris)

Greek, meaning 'prince'.

Dino

Diminutive of Dean, meaning 'valley'.

Dion

Greek, short form of Dionysius, the Greek god of wine.

Dirk

Variant of Derek, meaning 'power of the tribe'.

Divakar

Sanskrit, meaning 'the sun'.

Dobbin

Diminutive of Robert, meaning 'bright fame'.

Dominic

Latin, meaning 'Lord'.

Donald

(alt. Don, Donal, Donaldo)

Gaelic, meaning 'great chief'.

Donato

Italian, meaning 'gift'.

Donnell

(alt. Donnie, Donny)

Gaelic, meaning 'world fighter'.

Donovan

Gaelic, meaning 'dark-haired chief'.

Doran

Gaelic, meaning 'exile'.

Dorian

Greek, meaning 'descendant of Doris'. Name of the title character in Oscar Wilde's *The Picture of Dorian Gray*.

D

Douglas
(alt. Dougal, Dougie)
Scottish, meaning 'black river'.

Doyle
Irish, meaning 'foreigner'.

Draco
Latin, meaning 'dragon'. Made popular by the character Draco Malfoy in the Harry Potter series.

Drake
Greek, meaning 'dragon'.

Drew
Shortened form of Andrew, Greek, meaning 'man' or 'warrior'.

Dryden
English, meaning 'dry town'.

Dudley
Old English, meaning 'people's field'. Also a town in the West Midlands, and the name of Harry Potter's cousin.

Duff
Gaelic, meaning 'swarthy'.

Duke
Latin, meaning 'leader'.

Duncan
Scottish, meaning 'dark warrior'.

Dustin
(alt. Dusty)
French, meaning 'brave warrior'.

Dwayne
Irish Gaelic, meaning 'swarthy'.

Dwight
Flemish, meaning 'blond'.

Dwyer
Gaelic, meaning 'dark wise one'.

Dyani
Native American, meaning 'eagle'.

Dylan
(alt. Dillon)
Welsh, meaning 'son of the sea'.

 Boys' names

Eagan

Irish, meaning 'fiery'.

Eamon

(alt. Eames)

Irish, meaning 'wealthy protector'.

Earl

(alt. Earle, Errol)

English, meaning 'nobleman, warrior, prince'.

Ebb

Shortened form of Ebenezer, meaning 'stone of help'.

Ebenezer

Hebrew, meaning 'stone of help'.

Ed

(alt. Edd, Eddie, Eddy)

Shortened form of Edward, meaning 'wealthy guard'.

Edgar

(alt. Elgar)

Old English, meaning 'wealthy spear'.

Edison

English, meaning 'son of Edward'.

Edmund

English, meaning 'wealthy protector'.

Edric

Old English, meaning 'rich and powerful'.

E

Edsel
Old German, meaning 'noble'.

Edward
(alt. Eduardo)
Old English, meaning 'wealthy guard'.

Edwin
English, meaning 'wealthy friend'.

Efrain
Hebrew, meaning 'fruitful'.

Egan
Irish, meaning 'fire'.

Eilif
(alt. Elif, Eilyg, Elyf)
Norse, meaning 'immortal'.

Einar
Old Norse, meaning 'battle leader'.

Eladio
Greek, meaning 'Greek'.

Elam
Hebrew, meaning 'eternal'.

Elbert
Old English, meaning 'famous'.

Eldon
Old English, meaning 'Ella's hill'.

Eldred
(alt. Eldridge)
Old English, meaning 'old venerable counsel'.

Elgin
Old English, meaning 'high minded'.

Eli
(alt. Eliah)
Hebrew, meaning 'high'.

Elias
(alt. Elijah)
Hebrew, meaning 'the Lord is my God'.

Elio
Spanish, meaning 'the Lord is my God'.

Ellery
Old English, meaning 'elder tree'.

Elliott
Spanish, variant of Elio, meaning 'the Lord is my God'.

Ellis
Welsh, variant of Elio, meaning 'the Lord is my God'.

E

Ellison
English, meaning 'son of Ellis'.

Elmer
(alt. Elmo)
Old English, meaning 'noble';
Arabic, meaning 'aristocratic'.

Elmo
(alt. Ellmo, Elmon)
Greek, meaning 'gregarious'. One
of the characters in the children's
TV series *Sesame Street*.

Elon
Hebrew, meaning 'oak tree'.

Elroy
French, meaning 'king'.

Elton
Old English, meaning 'Ella's town'.

Elvin
English, meaning 'elf-like'.

Elvis
Figure in Norse mythology. Made
famous by the singer Elvis Presley.

Emanuel
Hebrew, meaning 'God is with us'.

Emeric
German, meaning 'work rule'.

Emile
(alt. Emiliano, Emilio)
Latin, meaning 'eager'.

Emlyn
Welsh, name of town,
Newcastle Emlyn, in west
Wales.

Emmett
English, meaning 'universal'.

Emrys
Welsh, meaning 'immortal'.

Eneco
Spanish, meaning 'fiery one'.

Enoch
Hebrew, meaning 'dedicated'.

Enrico
(alt. Enrique)
Italian, form of Henry, meaning
'home ruler'.

Enzo
Italian, short for Lorenzo,
meaning 'laurel'.

E

Eoghan
(alt. Eoin)
Irish form of Owen, meaning 'well born' or 'noble'.

Eoin
Irish, meaning 'God is gracious'.

Ephron
(alt. Effron)
Hebrew, meaning 'dust'.

Erasmo
(alt. Erasmus)
Greek, meaning 'to love'.

Eric
Old Norse, meaning 'ruler'.

Ernest
(alt. Ernesto, Ernie, Ernst)
Old German, meaning 'serious'.

Errol
English, meaning 'boar wolf'.

Erskine
Scottish, meaning 'high cliff'. Also a place in Scotland.

Erwin
Old English, meaning 'boar friend'.

Eryx
Greek, meaning 'boxer'.

Ethan
(alt. Etienne)
Hebrew, meaning 'long lived'.

Eugene
Greek, meaning 'well born'.

Evan
Welsh, meaning 'God is good'.

Everard
Old English, meaning 'strong boar'.

Everett
English, meaning 'strong boar'.

Ewald
(alt. Ewan, Ewell)
Old English, from Owen, meaning 'well born' or 'noble'.

Exton
English, meaning 'on the River Exe'.

Ezra
Hebrew, meaning 'helper'. Associated with the poet Ezra Pound.

 Boys' names

Faber
(alt. Fabir)

Latin, meaning 'blacksmith'.

Fabian
(alt. Fabien, Fabio)

Latin, meaning 'one who grows beans'.

Fabrice
(alt. Fabrizio)

Latin, meaning 'works with his hands'.

Faisal
Arabic, meaning 'resolute'.

Falco
(alt. Falcon, Falconer, Falke)

Latin, meaning 'falconer'.

Faron
Spanish, meaning 'pharaoh'.

Farrell
Gaelic, meaning 'hero'.

Faulkner
Latin, from 'falcon'.

Faustino
Latin, meaning 'fortunate'.

Fela
(alt. Felah, Fella, Fellah)

African, meaning 'a man who is warlike'. The name of the famous Nigerian musician Fela Kuti.

F

Names of poets

Andrew (Marvell)
Geoffrey (Chaucer)
Hugo (Williams)
John (Donne, Keats, Milton)
Percy (Bysshe Shelley)
Robert (Burns)
Siegfried (Sassoon)
Ted (Hughes)
Walt (Whitman)
William (Blake, Wordsworth)

Felipe
(alt. Filippo)
Spanish, meaning 'lover of horses'.

Felix
(alt. Felice)
Italian/Latin, meaning 'happy'.

Fennel
Latin, name of a herb.

Ferdinand
(alt. Fernando)
Old German, meaning 'bold voyager'.

Fergus
(alt. Ferguson)
Gaelic, meaning 'supreme man'.

Ferris
Gaelic, meaning 'rock'.

Fiachra
Irish, meaning 'raven'.

Fidel
Latin, meaning 'faithful'.

Finbar
Gaelic, meaning 'fair head'.

Finian

Gaelic, meaning 'fair'.

Finlay

(alt. Finley, Finn)

Gaelic, meaning 'fair haired courageous one'.

Finnegan

Gaelic, meaning 'fair'.

Fintan

Gaelic, meaning 'little fair one'.

Fitzroy

English, meaning 'the king's son'.

Flavio

Latin, meaning 'yellow hair'.

Florencio

(alt. Florentino)

Latin, meaning 'from Florence'.

Florian

(alt. Florin)

Slavic/Latin, meaning 'flower'.

Floyd

Welsh, meaning 'grey haired'.

Flynn

Gaelic, meaning 'with a ruddy complexion'.

Forbes

(alt. Forbs, Forb, Forbe)

Gaelic, meaning 'of the field'.

Fortunato

Italian, meaning 'lucky'.

Foster

Old English, meaning 'woodsman'.

Fotini

(alt. Fotis)

Greek, meaning 'light'.

Francesco

(alt. Francis, Francisco, Franco, François)

Latin, meaning 'from France'.

Frank

(alt. Frankie, Franklin, Franz)

Middle English, meaning 'free landholder'.

F

Fraser

Scottish, meaning 'of the forest men'.

Frederick

(alt. Freddie, Fred)

Old German, meaning 'peaceful ruler'.

Furman

Old German, meaning 'ferryman'.

Fyfe

(alt. Fife, Fyffes)

Scottish, meaning 'from Fifeshire'.

Boys' names

Gabe

Hebrew, shortened form of Gabriel, meaning 'hero of God'.

Gabino

Latin, meaning 'God is my strength'.

Gabriel

Hebrew, meaning 'hero of God'. One of the archangels.

Gael

English, old reference to the Celts.

Gaius

(alt. Gaeus)

Latin, meaning 'rejoicing'.

Galen

Greek, meaning 'healer'.

Galileo

Italian, meaning 'from Galilee'.

Ganesh

Hindi, meaning 'Lord of the throngs'. One of the Hindu deities.

Gannon

Irish, meaning 'fair skinned'.

Gareth

(alt. Garth)

Welsh, meaning 'gentle'.

Garfield

Old English, meaning 'spear field'. Also the name of the cartoon cat.

G

Garland

English, as in 'garland of flowers'.

Garnet

English, precious stone red in colour.

Garrett

Old German, meaning 'spear' or 'ruler'.

Garth

(alt. Garthe, Gart, Garte)

Norse, meaning 'enclosure'.

Gary

(alt. Garry, Geary)

Old English, meaning 'spear'.

Gaspar

(alt. Gaspard)

Persian, meaning 'treasurer'.

Gaston

From the Gascony region in the south of France.

Gavin

(alt. Gawain)

Scottish/Welsh, meaning 'little falcon'.

Gene

Greek, shortened form of Eugene, meaning 'well born'.

Genkei

Japanese, meaning 'honoured'.

Gennaro

Italian, meaning 'of Janus'.

Geoffrey

Old German, meaning 'peace'.

George

(alt. Giorgio)

Greek, meaning 'farmer'.

Gerald

(alt. Geraldo, Gerard, Gerardo, Gerhard)

Old German, meaning 'spear ruler'.

Geronimo

Italian, meaning 'sacred name'.

Gerry

English, meaning 'independent'.

G

Gert
Old German, meaning 'strong spear'.

Gervase
Old German, meaning 'with honour'.

Giacomo
Italian, meaning 'God's son'.

Gibson
English, meaning 'son of Gilbert'.

Gideon
Hebrew, meaning 'tree cutter'.

Gilbert
(alt. Gilberto)
French, meaning 'bright promise'.

Giles
Greek, meaning 'small goat'.

Gino
Italian, meaning 'well born'.

Giovanni
Italian form of John, meaning 'God is gracious'.

Giri
(alt. Gririe, Giry, Girey)
Indian, meaning 'from the mountain'.

Giulio
Italian, meaning 'youthful'.

Giuseppe
Italian form of Joseph, meaning 'Jehovah increases'.

Glen
English, from the word 'glen'.

Glyn
Welsh form of Glen.

Godfrey
German, meaning 'peace of God'.

Gordon
Gaelic, meaning 'large fortification'.

Gottlieb
German, meaning 'good love'.

Gower
Area on the Welsh coast.

Graeme
(alt. Graham)
English, meaning 'gravelled area'.

Grant
English, from the word 'grant'.

Granville
English, meaning 'gravelly town'.

Gray
(alt. Grey)
English, from the word 'gray'.

Grayson
English, meaning 'son of gray'.

Green
English, from the word 'green'.

Greg
(alt. Gregorio, Gregory, Grieg)
English, meaning 'watcher'.

Griffin
English, from the word 'griffin'.

Groves
English, meaning 'inhabits near grove of trees'.

Guido
Italian, meaning 'guide'.

Guillaume
French form of William, meaning 'strong protector'.

Gulliver
English, meaning 'glutton'.

Gunther
German, meaning 'warrior'.

Gurpreet
Indian, meaning 'love of the teacher'.

Gustave
(alt. Gus)
Scandinavian, meaning 'royal staff'.

Guy
English, from the word 'guy'.

Grylfi
(alt. Gylfie, Gylfee, Gylffi)
Scandinavian, meaning 'king'.

Gwyn
Welsh, meaning 'white'.

 **Boys' names**

Habib
Arabic, meaning 'beloved one'.

Hackett
(alt. Hacket, Hackit, Hackitt)
German, meaning 'small hacker'.

Haden
(alt. Haiden)
English, meaning 'hedged valley'.

Hades
Greek, meaning 'sightless'. Name of the underworld in Greek mythology.

Hadrian
From Hadria, a north Italian city.

Hadwin
Old English, meaning 'friend in war'.

Hakeem
Arabic, meaning 'wise and insightful'.

Hal
(alt. Hale, Hallie)
English, nickname for Henry, meaning 'home ruler'.

Halim
Arabic, meaning 'gentle'.

Hallam
Old English, meaning 'the valley'.

Hamid
Arabic, meaning 'praiseworthy'.

H

Hamilton
Old English, meaning 'flat topped hill'.

Hamish
Scottish form of James, meaning 'he who supplants'.

Hamlet
(alt. Hamlett, Hammet, Hamnet)
German, meaning 'village'. A variation of the Danish Amleth, and often associated with Shakespeare's tragedy *Hamlet*.

Hampus
Swedish form of Homer, meaning 'pledge'.

Hamza
Arabic, meaning 'lamb'.

Han
(alt. Hannes, Hans)
Scandinavian, meaning 'the Lord is gracious'.

Hanif
(alt. Haneef, Haneaf, Haneif)
Arabic, meaning 'devout'.

Hank
German, form of Henry, meaning 'home ruler'.

Hansel
German, meaning 'the Lord is gracious'.

Hardy
English, meaning 'tough'. Often associated with the author Thomas Hardy.

Harlan
English, meaning 'dweller by the boundary wood'.

Names from ancient Greece

Aeschylus
Erasmus
Hieronymus
Homer
Jason
Leonidas
Nikolaos
Sophocles
Theodore

H

Harland
Old English, meaning 'army land'.

Harley
Old English, meaning 'hare meadow'.

Harmon
Old German, meaning 'soldier'.

Harold
Scandinavian, meaning 'army ruler'.

Harry
Old German, form of Henry, meaning 'home ruler'.

Hart
Old English, meaning 'stag'.

Harvey
Old English, meaning 'strong and worthy'.

Haskell
Hebrew, meaning 'intellect'.

Hassan
Arabic, meaning 'handsome'.

Haydn
(alt. Hayden, Haydon)
Old English, meaning 'hedged valley'.

Heart
English, from the word 'heart'.

Heath
English, meaning 'heath' or 'moor'.

Heathcliff
English, meaning 'cliff near a heath'. Made famous by Emily Bronte's novel *Wuthering Heights*.

Heber
Hebrew, meaning 'partner'.

Hector
Greek, meaning 'steadfast'.

Henry
(alt. Henri, Hendrik, Hendrix)
Old German, meaning 'home ruler'.

Henson
English, meaning 'son of Henry'.

H

Herbert
(alt. Bert, Herb)
Old German, meaning 'illustrious warrior'.

Heriberto
Spanish variant of Herbert, meaning 'illustrious warrior'.

Herman
(alt. Herminio, Hermon)
Old German, meaning 'soldier'.

Hermes
Greek, meaning 'messenger'. The messenger of the gods in Greek mythology.

Herschel
Yiddish, meaning 'deer'.

Hezekiah
Hebrew, meaning 'God gives strength'.

Hideki
Japanese, meaning 'excellent trees'.

Hideo
Japanese, meaning 'excellent name'.

Hilario
Latin, meaning 'cheerful, happy'.

Hilary
English, meaning 'cheerful'.

Hillel
Hebrew, meaning 'greatly praised'.

Hilliard
Old German, meaning 'battle guard'.

Hilton
Old English, meaning 'hill settlement'.

Hiram
Hebrew, meaning 'exalted brother'.

Hiro
Spanish, meaning 'sacred name'.

Hiroshi
Japanese, meaning 'generous'.

Hirsch
Yiddish, meaning 'deer'.

Hobart

English, meaning 'bright and shining intellect'.

Hodge

English, meaning 'son of Roger'.

Hogan

Gaelic, meaning 'youth'.

Holden

English, meaning 'deep valley'.

Hollis

Old English, meaning 'holly tree'.

Homer

Greek, meaning 'pledge'. Name of the Greek poet, and the TV character Homer Simpson.

Honorius

Latin, meaning 'honourable'.

Horace

Latin, name of the Roman poet.

Houston

Old English, meaning 'Hugh's town'. Also a city in the state of Texas, USA.

Howard

Old English, meaning 'noble watchman'.

Howell

Welsh, meaning 'eminent and remarkable'.

Hoyt

Norse, meaning 'spirit' or 'soul'.

Hristo

From Christo, meaning 'follower of Christ'.

Hubbell

(alt. Hubble)

English, meaning 'brave hearted'.

Hubert

German, meaning 'bright and shining intellect'.

Hudson

Old English, meaning 'son of Hugh'.

Hugh

Old German, meaning 'soul, mind and intellect'.

Hugo

German, meaning 'bright in mind and spirit'.

Humbert

Old German, meaning 'famous giant'. Be warned: it's the name and surname of the paedophile protagonist of Vladimir Nabokov's *Lolita*.

Humphrey

Old German, meaning 'peaceful warrior'.

Hunter

English, from the word 'hunter'.

Hurley

Gaelic, meaning 'sea tide'.

Huxley

Old English, meaning 'Hugh's meadow'.

Hyrum

Hebrew, meaning 'exalted brother'.

Surnames as first names

Campbell	Lewis
Connor	Jackson
Cooper	Taylor
Hamilton	Walker
Harrison	Watson

Boys' names

Iago
Spanish, meaning 'he who supplants'. Name of the villain in Shakespeare's *Othello*.

Ian
(alt. Ion)

Gaelic, variant of John, meaning 'God is gracious'.

Ianto
Welsh, meaning 'gift of God'.

Ibaad
Arabic, meaning 'a believer in God'.

Ibrahim
Arabic, meaning 'father of many'.

Ichabod
Hebrew, meaning 'glory is good'.

Ichiro
Japanese, meaning 'firstborn son'.

Idan
Hebrew, meaning 'place in time'.

Idris
Welsh, meaning 'fiery leader'.

Ifan
Welsh variant of John, meaning 'God is gracious'.

I

Ignacio

Latin, meaning 'ardent' or 'burning'.

Ignatz

German, meaning 'fiery'.

Igor

Russian, meaning 'Ing's soldier'.

Ikaika

Hawaiian, meaning 'strong'.

Ike

Hebrew, short for Isaac, meaning 'laughter'.

Girls' names for boys (male spellings)

Darcy
Gene (or Jean in France)
Kay
Kelly
Kelsey
Madison
Nat
Paris
Sandy
Sasha

Iku

Japanese, meaning 'nourishing'.

Ilan

Hebrew, meaning 'tree'.

Ilias

Variant of Hebrew Elijah, meaning 'the Lord is my God'.

Imanol

Hebrew, meaning 'God is with us'.

Indiana

Latin, meaning 'from India'. Also a state in the USA.

Indigo

English, describing a deep blue colour.

Indio

Spanish, meaning 'indigenous people'.

Ingo

Danish, meaning 'meadow'.

Inigo

Spanish, meaning 'fiery'.

Ioannis

Greek, meaning 'the Lord is gracious'.

Iovianno

Native American, meaning 'yellow hawk'.

Ira

Hebrew, meaning 'full grown and watchful'.

Irvin

(alt. Irving, Irwin)

Gaelic, meaning 'green and fresh water'.

Isaac

(alt. Isaak)

Hebrew, meaning 'laughter'.

Isadore

(alt. Isidore, Isidro)

Greek, meaning 'gift of Isis'.

Isai

(alt. Isaiah, Isaias, Izaiah)

Arabic, meaning 'protection and security'.

Iser

Yiddish, meaning 'God wrestler'.

Place names

Austin
Carson
Chester
Glen
Jericho
London
Paris
Seymour
Whitley
Windsor

Ishedus

Native American, meaning 'on top'.

Ishmael

(alt. Ismael)

Hebrew, meaning 'God listens'.

Israel

Hebrew, meaning 'God perseveres'. Also the name of the country.

Istvan

Hungarian variant of Stephen, meaning 'crowned'.

Itai

Hebrew, meaning 'the Lord is with me'.

Ivan

Hebrew, meaning 'God is gracious'.

Ivanhoe

Russian, meaning 'God is gracious'. Also name of the novel by Walter Scott.

Ivey

English, variant of Ivy.

Ivo

French, from the word 'yves', meaning 'yew tree'.

Ivor

Scandinavian, meaning 'yew'.

Ivory

English, from the word 'ivory'.

Izar

Basque, meaning 'star'.

Boys' names

Jabari
Swahili, meaning 'valiant'.

Jabez
Hebrew, meaning 'borne in pain'.

Jabulani
(alt. Jabulanie, Jabulany, Jabulaney)
African, meaning 'happy one'.

Jace
(alt. Jaece, Jase, Jayce)
Hebrew, meaning 'healer'.

Jacek
African, meaning 'hyacinth'.

Jacinto
African, meaning 'hyacinth'.

Jack
(alt. Jackie, Jacky)
From the Hebrew John, meaning 'God is gracious'. The UK's most popular boy's name for 14 years until 2011.

Jackson
English, meaning 'son of Jack'.

Jaco
Hebrew, from Jacob, meaning 'he who supplants'.

Jacob
(alt. Jacobo, Jago)
Hebrew, meaning 'he who supplants'.

Jacques
French form of Jack, meaning 'God is gracious'.

J

Jaden
(alt. Jaden, Jadyn, Jaeden, Jaiden, Jaidyn, Jayden, Jaydin)
Hebrew, meaning 'Jehovah has heard'.

Jaegar
(alt. Jager, Jaecer, Jaegar)
German, meaning 'mighty hunter'.

Jafar
Arabic, meaning 'stream'.

Jagger
Old English, meaning 'one who cuts'.

Jaheem
(alt. Jaheim)
Hebrew, meaning 'raised up'.

Jahir
Hindi, meaning 'jewel'.

Jaime
Variant of James, meaning 'he who supplants'. 'J'aime' is French for 'I love'.

Jair
(alt. Jairo)
Hebrew, meaning 'God enlightens'.

Jake
Shortened form of Jacob, meaning 'he who supplants'.

Jalen
Greek, meaning 'healer' or 'tranquil'.

Jali
Swahili, meaning 'musician'.

Jalon
Greek, meaning 'healer' or 'tranquil'.

Jamaal
(alt. Jamal)
Arabic, meaning 'handsome'.

Jamar
(alt. Jamarcus, Jamari, Jamarion, Jamir)
Modern variant of Jamaal, meaning 'handsome'.

Jamel
Arabic, meaning 'handsome'.

James

English, meaning 'he who supplants'.

Jameson

(alt. Jamison)

English, meaning 'son of James'.

Jamie

(alt. Jamey, Jaimie)

Nickname for James, meaning 'he who supplants'.

Jamil

Arabic, meaning 'handsome'.

Short names

Al
Ben
Dev
Ed
Jo
Kev
Max
Rob
Sam
Ty

Jamin

Hebrew, meaning 'son of the right hand'.

Jan

(alt. Janko, János)

Slavic, from John, meaning 'the Lord is gracious'.

Janesh

Hindi, meaning 'leader of people'.

Janus

Latin, meaning 'gateway'. Roman god of doors, beginnings and endings.

Japhet

(alt. Japheth)

Hebrew, meaning 'comely'.

Jaquez

French, form of Jacques, meaning 'God is gracious'.

Jared

(alt. Jarem, Jaren, Jaret, Jarod, Jarrod)

Hebrew, meaning 'descending'.

J

Jarlath

Gaelic, from Iarlaith, from Saint Iarfhlaith.

Jarom

Greek, meaning 'to raise and exalt'.

Jarrell

Variant of Gerald, meaning 'spear ruler'.

Jarrett

Old English, meaning 'spear-brave'.

Jarvis

Old German, meaning 'with honour'.

Jason

Greek, meaning 'healer'.

Jasper

Greek, meaning 'treasure holder'.

Javen

Arabic, meaning 'youth'.

Javier

Spanish, meaning 'bright'.

Jaxon

From Jackson, meaning 'son of Jack'.

Jay

Latin, meaning 'jaybird'.

Jaylan

Greek, meaning 'healer'.

Jeevan

Indian, meaning 'life'.

Jefferson

English, meaning 'son of Jeffrey'.

Jeffrey
(alt. Jeff)

Old German, meaning 'peace'.

Jensen

Scandinavian, meaning 'son of Jan'.

Jeremiah
(alt. Jeremia, Jeremias, Jeremiya)

Hebrew, meaning 'the Lord exalts'.

J

Jeremy
(alt. Jem)
Hebrew, meaning 'the Lord exalts'.

Jeriah
Hebrew, meaning 'Jehovah has seen'.

Jericho
Arabic, meaning 'city of the moon'.

Jermaine
Latin, meaning 'brotherly'.

Jerome
Greek, meaning 'sacred name'.

Jerry
English, from Gerald, meaning 'spear ruler'.

Jesse
Hebrew, meaning 'the Lord exists'.

Jesus
Hebrew, meaning 'the Lord is Salvation' and the Son of God.

Jethro
Hebrew, meaning 'eminent'.

Jignesh
(alt. Jigneshe, Jygnesh, Jygneshe)
Indian, meaning 'curious'.

Jim
(alt. Jimmy)
From James, meaning 'he who supplants'.

Jiri
(alt. Jiro)
Greek, meaning 'farmer'.

Joachim
Hebrew, meaning 'established by God'.

Joah
(alt. João)
Hebrew, meaning 'God is gracious'.

Joaquin
Hebrew, meaning 'established by God'. Made famous by the actor Joaquin Phoenix.

J

Joe
(alt. Joey, Johan, Johannes, Jomar)
From Joseph, meaning 'Jehovah increases'.

Joel
Hebrew, meaning 'Jehovah is the Lord'.

John
Hebrew, meaning 'God is gracious'.

Johnny
(alt. Jon, Jonny)
From Jonathan, meaning 'gift of God'.

Jolyon
From Julian, meaning 'young'.

Jonah
Hebrew, meaning 'dove'.

Jonas
Hebrew, meaning 'dove'.

Jonathan
(alt. Johnathan, Johnathon, Jonathon, Jonty)
Hebrew, meaning 'God is gracious'.

Jordan
(alt. Jory, Judd)
Hebrew, meaning 'down-flowing'.

Jorge
From George, meaning 'farmer'.

José
Spanish variant of Joseph, meaning 'God increases'.

Joseph
(alt. Joss)
Hebrew, meaning 'God increases'.

Josh
Shortened form of Joshua, meaning 'God is salvation'.

Joshua
Hebrew, meaning 'God is salvation'.

Josiah
Hebrew, meaning 'God helps'.

Josué
Spanish variant of Joshua, meaning 'God is salvation'.

Jude

Hebrew, meaning 'praise' or 'thanks'. The title character in Hardy's novel *Jude the Obscure*.

Judson

Variant of Jude, meaning 'praise' or 'thanks'.

Jules

From Julian, meaning 'Jove's child'.

Julian

Greek, meaning 'Jove's child'.

Julien

French variant of Julian, meaning 'Jove's child'.

Julio

Spanish variant of Julian, meaning 'Jove's child'.

Julius

Latin, meaning 'youthful'.

Junior

Latin, meaning 'the younger one'.

'Bad boy' names

Arnie
Axel
Brett
Conan
Damian
Guy
Ivan
Preston
Stanley
Tyson

Jovan

Latin, meaning 'the supreme God'.

Joweese

Native American, meaning 'chirping bird'.

Joyce

Latin, meaning 'joy'.

Juan

Spanish variant of John, meaning 'God is gracious'.

Jubal

Hebrew, meaning 'ram's horn'.

J

Junius

Latin, meaning 'young'.

Jupiter

Latin, meaning 'the supreme God'. Jupiter was king of the Roman gods and the god of thunder. Jupiter is also the largest planet in the solar system.

Juraj

Hebrew, meaning 'God is my judge'.

Jurgen

Greek, meaning 'farmer'.

Justice

English, from the word 'justice'.

Justin

(alt. Justus)

Latin, meaning 'just and upright'.

Juwan

Hebrew, meaning 'the Lord is gracious'.

Famous male drummers

Dave (Grohl)

John (Bonham)

Keith (Moon)

Lars (Ulrich)

Mick (Fleetwood)

Phil (Collins)

Ringo (Starr)

Stewart (Copeland)

Tommy (Lee)

Travis (Barker)

K Boys' names

Kaamil

Arabic, meaning 'perfect'.

Kabelo

African, meaning 'gift'.

Kade

Scottish, meaning 'from the wetlands'.

Kadeem

Arabic, meaning 'one who serves'.

Kaden

(alt. Kadin, Kaeden, Kaedin, Kaiden)

Arabic, meaning 'companion'.

Kadir

Arabic, meaning 'capable and competent'.

Kafka

Czech, meaning 'bird-like'. Often associated with the author of *The Metamorphosis*.

Kahekili

Hawaiian, meaning 'the thunder'.

Kahlil

Arabic, meaning 'friend'.

Kai

Greek, meaning 'keeper of the keys'.

K

Kaito
Japanese, meaning 'ocean and sake dipper'.

Kalani
Hawaiian, meaning 'sky'.

Kale
German, meaning 'free man'.

Kaleb
(alt. Caleb)
Hebrew, meaning 'dog' or 'aggressive'.

Kalen
Gaelic, meaning 'uncertain'.

Kaleo
Hawaiian, meaning 'the voice'.

Kalil
Arabic, meaning 'friend'.

Kalvin
French, meaning 'bald'.

Kamari
Indian, meaning 'the enemy of desire'.

Kamden
English, meaning 'winding valley'.

Kamil
Arabic, meaning 'perfection'.

Kane
Gaelic, meaning 'little battler'.

Kani
Hawaiian, meaning 'sound'.

Kanye
African town. Made popular by rapper Kanye West.

Kareem
(alt. Karim)
Arabic, meaning 'generous'.

Karl
(alt. Karson)
Old German, meaning 'free man'.

Kasey
Irish, meaning 'alert'.

Kaspar
Persian, meaning 'treasurer'.

Kavon
Gaelic, meaning 'handsome'.

K

Kayden

Arabic, meaning 'companion'.

Kazimierz

Polish, meaning 'declares peace'.

Kazuki

Japanese, meaning 'radiant hope'.

Kazuo

Japanese, meaning 'harmonious man'.

Keagan

(alt. Keegan, Kegan)

Gaelic, meaning 'small flame'.

Keane

Gaelic, meaning 'fighter'.

Keanu

Hawaiian, meaning 'breeze'. Made famous by the actor Keanu Reeves.

Keary

Gaelic, meaning 'black-haired'.

Keaton

English, meaning 'place of hawks'.

Keefe

(alt. Keef, Kief, Kiefe)

Gaelic, meaning 'beautiful and graceful'.

Keeler

Gaelic, meaning 'beautiful and graceful'.

Keenan

(alt. Kenan)

Gaelic, meaning 'little ancient one'.

Keiji

Japanese, meaning 'govern with discretion'.

Keir

Gaelic, meaning 'dark-haired' or 'dark-skinned'.

Keith

Gaelic, meaning 'woodland'.

Kekoa

Hawaiian, meaning 'brave one' or 'soldier'.

Kelby

Old English, meaning 'farmhouse near the stream'.

K

Kell
(alt. *Kellan, Kellen, Kelley, Kelly, Kiel*)

Norse, meaning 'spring'.

Kelsey
Old English, meaning 'victorious ship'.

Kelton
Old English, meaning 'town of the keels'.

Kelvin
Old English, meaning 'friend of ships'.

Kemenes
Hungarian, meaning 'maker of furnaces'.

Ken
Shortened form of Kenneth, meaning 'born of fire'.

Kendal
Old English, meaning 'the Kent river valley'.

Kendon
Old English, meaning 'brave guard'.

Kendrick
Gaelic, meaning 'royal ruler'.

Kenelm
Old English, meaning 'bold'.

Kenji
Japanese, meaning 'intelligent second son'.

Kennedy
Gaelic, meaning 'helmet head'.

Kenneth
(alt. *Kenney*)

Gaelic, meaning 'born of fire'.

Kennison
English, meaning 'son of Kenneth'.

Kent
From the English county.

Kenton
English, meaning 'town of Ken'.

Kenya
From the country in Africa.

Kenzo
Japanese, meaning 'wise'.

Дарья - Даша
Sophia
Ulgana
Darina
Stefania
Polina
Jelena

Steffany

K

Keola
Hawaiian, meaning 'life'.

Keon
(alt. Keoni)
Hawaiian, meaning 'gracious'.

Kepler
German, meaning 'hat maker'.

Kermit
(alt. Kerwin)
Gaelic, meaning 'without envy'. Associated with Kermit the Frog, the Muppets character.

Kerr
English, meaning 'wetland'.

Keshav
Indian, meaning 'beautiful-haired'.

Kevin
Gaelic, meaning 'handsome beloved'.

Khalid
(alt. Khalif, Khalil)
Arabic, meaning 'immortal'.

Kian
(alt. Keyon, Kyan)
Irish, meaning 'ancient'.

Kiefer
German, meaning 'barrel maker'.

Literary names

Charlie (*Charlie and the Chocolate Factory*, Roald Dahl)
Christopher (*Now We Are Six*, A. A. Milne)
David (*David Copperfield*, Charles Dickens)
Gabriel (*Far from the Madding Crowd*, Thomas Hardy)
Dorian (*The Picture of Dorian Gray*, Oscar Wilde)
Ishmael (*Moby Dick*, Herman Melville)
James (*James and the Giant Peach*, Roald Dahl)
Karin (*The Buddha of Suburbia*, Hanif Kureishi)
Phileas (*Around the World in Eighty Days*, Jules Verne)
Richard (*The Beach*, Alex Garland)
Winston (*Nineteen Eighty-Four*, George Orwell)

K

Kieran
(alt. Kyron)
Gaelic, meaning 'black'.

Kijana
African, meaning 'youth'.

Kilby
From the English 'Cilebi', a place in Leicestershire.

Kilian
Irish, meaning 'bright headed'.

Kimani
African, meaning 'beautiful and sweet'.

King
English, from the word 'king'.

Kingsley
English, meaning 'the king's meadow'.

Kirby
German, meaning 'settlement by a church'.

Kirk
Old German, meaning 'church'.

Klaus
German, meaning 'victorious'.

Knightley
(alt. Knightly)
English, meaning 'of the knight's meadows'. Surname of the hero in Jane Austen's *Emma*.

Kobe
(alt. Koda, Kody)
Japanese, meaning 'a Japanese city'.

Kofi
Ghanaian, meaning 'born on Friday'.

Kohana
Japanese, meaning 'little flower'.

Kojo
Ghanaian, meaning 'Monday'.

Kolby
Norse, meaning 'settlement'.

Korbin
Gaelic, meaning 'a steep hill'.

Kramer

German, meaning 'shopkeeper'.

Kris

(alt. Krish)

From Christopher, meaning 'bearing Christ inside'.

Kurt

German, meaning 'courageous advice'.

Kurtis

French, meaning 'courtier'.

Kwame

Ghanaian, meaning 'born on Saturday'.

Kyden

English, meaning 'narrow little fire'.

Kylan

(alt. Kyle, Kyleb, Kyler)

Gaelic, meaning 'narrow and straight'.

Kyllion

Irish, meaning 'war'.

Kyree

From Cree, a Canadian tribe.

Kyros

Greek, meaning 'legitimate power'.

English and Scottish royalty

Alexander	James
Charles	Richard
Edward	Robert
George	Stephen
Henry	William

L Boys' names

Laban

Hebrew, meaning 'white'.

Lachlan

Gaelic, meaning 'from the land of lakes'.

Lacy

Old French, after the place in France.

Laertes

English, meaning 'adventurous'. Ophelia's brother in Shakespeare's *Hamlet*.

Lalit

Hindi, meaning 'beautiful'.

Lamar

Old German, meaning 'water'.

Lambert

Scandinavian, meaning 'land brilliant'.

Lambros

Greek, meaning 'brilliant and radiant'.

Lamont

Old Norse, meaning 'law man'.

Lance

French, meaning 'land'.

Lancelot

Variant of Lance, meaning 'land'. The name of one of the Knights of the Round Table.

Landen

(*alt. Lando, Landon, Langdon*)

English, meaning 'long hill'.

Landyn

Welsh variant of Landen, meaning 'long hill'.

Lane

(alt. Layne)

English, from the word 'lanel'.

Lang

Norse, meaning 'long meadow'.

Lannie

(alt. Lanny)

German, meaning 'precious'.

Larkin

Gaelic, meaning 'rough' or 'fierce'.

Laron

French, meaning 'thief'.

Larry

Latin, variant of Lawrence, meaning 'man from Laurentum'.

Lars

Scandinavian variant of Lawrence, meaning 'man from Laurentum'.

Lasse

Finnish, meaning 'girl'. (Still, ironically, a boy's name.)

Laszlo

Hungarian, meaning 'glorious rule'.

Lathyn

Latin, meaning 'fighter'.

Latif

Arabic, meaning 'gentle'.

Laurel

Latin, meaning 'bay'.

Laurent

French form of Lawrence, meaning 'man from Laurentum'.

Lawrence

Latin, meaning 'man from Laurentum'.

Lazarus

Hebrew, meaning 'God is my help'.

Leandro

Latin, meaning 'lion man'.

Lear

German, meaning 'of the meadow'.

Lee

(alt. Leigh)

Old English, meaning 'meadow' or 'valley'.

Leib

German, meaning 'love'.

Leif

Scandinavian, meaning 'heir'.

Leith

From the name of a place in Scotland.

Lennox

(alt. Lenny)

Gaelic, meaning 'with many elm trees'.

Leo

Latin, meaning 'lion'.

Leon

Latin, meaning 'lion'.

Leonard

Old German, meaning 'lion strength'.

Leopold

German, meaning 'brave people'.

Leroy

French, meaning 'king'.

Lesley

(alt. Les)

Scottish, meaning 'holly garden'.

Lester

English, meaning 'from Leicester'.

Lewis

French, meaning 'renowned fighter'.

Lex

English variant of Alexander, meaning 'defending men'.

Liam

German, meaning 'helmet'.

Lincoln

English, meaning 'lake colony'.

L

Lindsay
Scottish, meaning 'linden tree'.

Linus
Latin, meaning 'lion'.

Lionel
English, meaning 'lion'.

Llewellyn
Welsh, meaning 'like a lion'.

Lloyd
Welsh, meaning 'grey-haired and sacred'.

Logan
Gaelic, meaning 'hollow'.

Lonnie
English, meaning 'lion strength'.

Lorcan
Gaelic, meaning 'little fierce one'.

Louis
(alt. Lou, Louie, Luigi, Luis)
German, meaning 'famous warrior'.

Lucas
(alt. Lukas, Luca)
English, meaning 'man from Luciana'.

Lucian
(alt. Lucio)
Latin, meaning 'light'.

Ludwig
German, meaning 'famous fighter'.

Luke
(alt. Luc, Luka)
Latin, meaning 'from Lucanus'.

Lupe
Latin, meaning 'wolf'.

Luther
German, meaning 'soldier of the people'.

Lyle
French, meaning 'the island'.

Lyn
(alt. Lyndon)
Spanish, meaning 'pretty'.

Boys' names

Mabon

(alt. Maban, Mabery)

Welsh, meaning 'our son'.

Mac

(alt. Mack, Mackie)

Scottish, meaning 'son of'.

Macaulay

Scottish, meaning 'son of the phantom'.

Mace

English, meaning 'heavy staff' or 'club'.

Mackenzie

Scottish, meaning 'the fair one'.

Mackland

Scottish, meaning 'land of Mac'.

Macon

French, name of towns in France and Georgia.

Macsen

Scottish, meaning 'son of Mac'.

Madden

Irish, meaning 'descendant of the hound'.

Maddox

English, meaning 'good' or 'generous'.

Madison

(alt. Madsen)

Irish, meaning 'son of Madden'.

159

Mads

Shortened form of Madden, meaning 'descendant of the hound'.

Magnus

(alt. Manus)

Latin, meaning 'great'.

Maguire

Gaelic, meaning 'son of the beige one'.

Mahabala

Indian, meaning 'great strength'.

Mahesh

Hindi, meaning 'great ruler'.

Mahir

Arabic, meaning 'skilful'.

Mahlon

Hebrew, meaning 'sickness'.

Mahmoud

Arabic, meaning 'praiseworthy'.

Mahoney

Irish, meaning 'bear'.

Major

English, from the word 'major'.

Makal

From Michael, meaning 'close to God'.

Makani

Hawaiian, meaning 'wind'.

Makis

Hebrew, meaning 'gift from God'.

Mako

Hebrew, meaning 'God is with us'.

Malachi

(alt. Malachy)

Irish, meaning 'messenger of God'.

Malcolm

English, meaning 'Columba's servant'.

Mali

Arabic, meaning 'full and rich'.

Manfred

Old German, meaning 'man of peace'.

Manish

English, meaning 'manly'.

Manley

English, meaning 'manly and brave'.

Mannix

Gaelic, meaning 'little monk'.

Manoi

(alt. Manos)

Japanese, meaning 'love springing from intellect'.

Manuel

Hebrew, meaning 'God is with us'.

Manzi

Italian, meaning 'steer'.

Marc

(alt. Marco, Marcos, Marcus, Markel)

French, meaning 'from the god Mars'.

Marcel

(alt. Marcelino, Marcello)

French, meaning 'little warrior'.

Marek

Polish variant of Mark, meaning 'from the god Mars'.

Mariano

Latin, meaning 'from the god Mars'.

Mario

(alt. Marius)

Latin, meaning 'manly'.

Mark

English, meaning 'from the god Mars'.

Marley

(alt. Marlin)

Old English, meaning 'meadow near the lake'.

Marlon

English, meaning 'like little hawk'. Famous as the forename of Marlon Brando.

Marshall

Old French, meaning 'caretaker of horses'.

Martin

Latin, meaning 'dedicated to Mars'.

M

Marty

Shortened form of Martin, meaning 'dedicated to Mars'.

Marvel

English, from the word 'marvel'.

Marvin

Welsh, meaning 'sea friend'.

Mason

English, from the word 'mason'.

Massimo

Italian, meaning 'greatest'.

Mathias

(alt. Matthias)

Hebrew, meaning 'gift of the Lord'.

Mathieu

French form of Matthew, meaning 'gift of God'.

Matthew

Hebrew, meaning 'gift of the Lord'.

Maurice

(alt. Mauricio)

Latin, meaning 'dark skinned' or 'Moorish'.

Maverick

American, meaning 'non-conformist leader'.

Max

(alt. Maxie, Maxim)

Latin, meaning 'greatest'.

Maximillian

Latin, meaning 'greatest'.

Maximino

Latin, meaning 'little Max'.

Maxwell

Latin, meaning 'Maccus' stream'.

Maynard

Old German, meaning 'brave'.

McArthur

Scottish, meaning 'son of Arthur'.

McCoy

Scottish, meaning 'son of Coy'.

Mearl

English, meaning 'my earl'.

Mederic
French, meaning 'doctor'.

Mekhi
African, meaning 'who is God?'.

Mel
Gaelic, meaning 'smooth brow'.

Melbourne
From the city in Australia.

Melchior
Persian, meaning 'king of the city'.

Melton
English, meaning 'town of Mel'.

Melva
Hawaiian, meaning 'plumeria'.

Melville
Scottish, meaning 'town of Mel'.

Melvin
(alt. Melvyn)
English, meaning 'smooth brow'.

Memphis
Greek, meaning 'established and beautiful'. Also the name of a city in the USA.

Mercer
English, from the word 'mercer'.

Merl
French, meaning 'blackbird'.

Merlin
Welsh, meaning 'sea fortress'.

Merrick
Welsh, meaning 'Moorish'.

Merrill
Gaelic, meaning 'shining sea'.

Merritt
English, from the word 'merit'.

Merton
Old English, meaning 'town by the lake'.

Meyer
Hebrew, meaning 'bright farmer'.

Michael

Hebrew, meaning 'resembles God'. One of the archangels.

Michalis

Greek form of Michael, meaning 'resembles God'.

Michel

French form of Michael, meaning 'resembles God'.

Michelangelo

Italian, meaning 'Michael's angel'. Name of the famous painter.

Michele

Italian form of Michael, meaning 'resembles God'.

Michio

Japanese, meaning 'a man with the strength of three thousand men'.

Mickey

Variant of Michael meaning 'resembles God'. Often associated with the Disney character Mickey Mouse.

Miguel

Spanish form of Michael, meaning 'resembles God'.

Mike

Shortened form of Michael, meaning 'resembles God'.

Miklos

Greek form of Michael, meaning 'resembles God'.

Milan

From the name of the Italian city.

Miles

(alt. Milo, Milos, Myles)

English, from the word 'miles'.

Milton

English, meaning 'miller's town'. Also the name of the poet John Milton.

Miro

Slavic, meaning 'peace'.

Misha

Russian, meaning 'who is like God'.

Football players

Aaron (Lennon)
Alan (Shearer)
Ashley (Cole)
David (Beckham)
Frank (Lampard)
Gary (Lineker)
Jack (Wilshere)
Joe (Cole)
John (Terry)
Rio (Ferdinand)
Scott (Parker)
Steven (Gerrard)
Wayne (Rooney)

Mitch

Shortened form of Mitchell, meaning 'who is like God'.

Mitchell

English, meaning 'who is like God'.

Modesto

Italian, meaning 'modest'.

Moe

Hebrew, meaning 'God's helmet'.

Mohamed

(alt. Mohammad, Mohamet, Mohammed)

Arabic, meaning 'praiseworthy'.

Monroe

Gaelic, meaning 'mouth of the river Rotha'.

Monserrate

Latin, meaning 'jagged mountain'.

Montague

French, meaning 'pointed hill'.

Montana

Latin, meaning 'mountain'. Also a state in the USA.

Monte

Italian, meaning 'mountain'.

Montgomery

Variant of Montague, meaning 'pointed hill'.

Monty

Shortened form of Montague, meaning 'pointed hill'.

M

Moody
English, from the word 'moody'.

Mordecai
Hebrew, meaning 'little man'.

Morgan
Welsh, meaning 'circling sea'.

Moritz
Latin, meaning 'dark skinned and Moorish'.

Moroccan
Arabic, meaning 'from Morocco'.

Morpheus
Greek, meaning 'shape'.

Morris
Welsh, meaning 'dark skinned and Moorish'.

Morrison
English, meaning 'son of Morris'.

Mortimer
French, meaning 'dead sea'.

Morton
Old English, meaning 'moor town'.

Moses
(alt. Moshe, Moshon)

Hebrew, meaning 'saviour'. In the Bible, Moses receives the Ten Commandments from God.

Moss
English, from the word 'moss'.

Muir
Gaelic, meaning 'of the moor'.

Mungo
Gaelic, meaning 'most dear'.

Murl
French, meaning 'blackbird'.

Murphy
Irish, meaning 'sea warrior'.

Murray
Gaelic, meaning 'lord and master'.

Mustafa
Arabic, meaning 'chosen'.

Myron
Greek, meaning 'myrrh'.

Mwita
African, meaning 'humourous one'.

 Boys' names

Nairn
Scottish, meaning 'alder-tree river'.

Najee
Arabic, meaning 'dear companion'.

Nakia
Arabic, meaning 'pure'.

Nakul
Indian, meaning 'mongoose'.

Naphtali
Hebrew, meaning 'wrestling'.

Napoleon
Italian, meaning 'man from Naples'. Name of the French general who became Emperor of France.

Narciso
Latin, from the myth of Narcissus, famous for drowning after falling in love with his own reflection.

Nash
English, meaning 'at the ash tree'.

Nasir
Arabic, meaning 'helper'.

N

Popular song names

Adam ('Adam's Son', Blink 182)
Al ('You Can Call Me Al', Paul Simon)
Alejandro ('Alejandro', Lady Gaga)
Anthony ('Movin' Out', Billy Joel)
Daniel ('Daniel', Elton John)
Frankie ('Frankie', Sister Sledge)
Jimmy ('Jimmy Mack', Martha Reeves and the Vandellas)
Joe ('Hey Joe', Jimi Hendrix)
Maxwell ('Maxwell's Silver Hammer', The Beatles)
Robert ('Doctor Robert', The Beatles)
William ('William It Was Really Nothing', The Smiths)

Nate
Hebrew, meaning 'God has given'.

Nathan
(alt. Nathaniel)
Hebrew, meaning 'God has given'.

Naval
Indian, meaning 'wonder'.

Naveen
Indian, meaning 'new'.

Neal
Irish, meaning 'champion'.

Ned
Nickname for Edward, meaning 'wealthy guard'.

Neftali
Hebrew, meaning 'struggling'.

Nehemiah
Hebrew, meaning 'comforter'.

Neil
(alt. Niall)
Irish, meaning 'champion'.

Neilson
Irish, meaning 'son of Neil'.

Nelson
Variant of Neil, meaning 'champion'.

Nemo
Latin, meaning 'nobody'.

Neo
Latin, meaning 'new'.

Nephi
Greek, meaning 'cloud'.

Nessim
Arabic, meaning 'breeze'.

Nestor
Greek, meaning 'traveller'.

Neville
Old French, meaning 'new village'.

Newland
(alt. Newlands, Newland, Neuland)
English, meaning 'from a new land'.

Newton
English, meaning 'new town'.

Nicholas
(alt. Niklas)
Greek, meaning 'victorious'.

Nick
(alt. Niko, Nikos, Nico)
Shortened form of Nicholas, meaning 'victorious'.

Nigel
Gaelic, meaning 'champion'.

Nikhil
Hindi, meaning 'whole' or 'entire'.

Nikita
Greek, meaning 'unconquered'. Also a girl's name.

Nikolai
Russian variant of Nicholas, meaning 'victorious'.

Nimrod
Hebrew, meaning 'we will rebel'.

Ninian
Gaelic, associated with the 5th-century saint of the same name.

Nissim
Hebrew, meaning 'wonderful things'.

N

Noah

Hebrew, meaning 'peaceful'.

Noel

French, meaning 'Christmas'.

Nolan

Gaelic, meaning 'champion'.

Norbert

Old German, meaning 'Northern brightness'.

Norman

Old German, meaning 'Northerner'.

Names of gods

Apollo (Music: Greek)
Eros (Love: Greek)
Hermes (Messenger of the
  gods: Greek)
Janus (Gates and Doors:
  Roman)
Mars (War: Roman)
Neptune (Sea: Roman)
Odin (Chief god: Norse)
Ra (Sun: Egyptian)
Thor (Thunder: Norse)

Normand

French, meaning 'from Normandy'.

Norris

Old French, meaning 'Northerner'.

Norton

English, meaning 'Northern town'.

Norval

French, meaning 'Northern town'.

Norwood

English, meaning 'Northern forest'.

Nova

Latin, meaning 'new'.

Nuno

Latin, meaning 'ninth'.

Nunzio

Italian, meaning 'messenger'.

Nyoka

African, meaning 'like a snake'.

 Boys' names

Oakley

English, meaning 'from the oak meadow'.

Obadiah

Hebrew, meaning 'God's worker'.

Obama

African, meaning 'crooked'. Made famous by the American President Barack Obama.

Obed

Hebrew, meaning 'servant of God'.

Popular French names

Alain	Jean
Alphonse	Louis
Gerard	Luc
Guy	Marc
Jacques	Mathieu

Oberon

Old German, meaning 'royal bear'. The Fairy King in *A Midsummer Night's Dream*.

Obie

Shortened form of Oberon, meaning 'royal bear'.

Obijulu

African, meaning 'one who has been consoled'.

Octave

(alt. Octavian, Octavio)

Latin, meaning 'eight'.

Oda

(alt. Odell, Odie, Odis)

Hebrew, meaning 'praise God'.

Ogden

Old English, meaning 'oak valley'.

Oisin

(alt. Ossian)

Celtic, meaning 'fawn'. The name of an ancient Irish poet.

Ola

Norse, meaning 'precious'.

Olaf

(alt. Olan)

Old Norse, meaning 'ancestor'.

Oleander

Hawaiian, meaning 'joyous'.

Oleg

(alt. Olen)

Russian, meaning 'holy'.

Olin

Russian, meaning 'rock'.

Oliver

Latin, meaning 'olive tree'. The UK's most popular boy's name in 2011.

Olivier

French form of Oliver, meaning 'olive tree'.

Ollie

Shortened form of Oliver, meaning 'olive tree'.

Omar

(alt. Omari, Omarion)

Arabic, meaning 'speaker'.

Ondrej

Czech, meaning 'manly'.

O

Ora

Latin, meaning 'hour'.

Oran

(alt. Oren, Orrin)

Gaelic, meaning 'light and pale'.

Orange

English, from the word 'orange'.

Orion

From the Greek hunter.

Orlando

(alt. Orlo)

Old German, meaning 'old land'. Name of a city in the USA.

Orpheus

Greek, meaning 'beautiful voice'.

Orrick

English, meaning 'sword ruler'.

Orson

Latin, meaning 'bear'.

Orville

Old French, meaning 'gold town'.

Osaka

From the Japanese city.

Osborne

Norse, meaning 'bear god'.

Oscar

Old English, meaning 'spear of the Gods'.

Osias

Hebrew, meaning 'salvation'.

Foreign alternatives

David – Dafydd, Davin
John – Jean, Giovanni, Juan
Michael – Miguel, Mikhail
Peter – Pedro, Pierre, Pyotr, Piers
Rory – Ruaridh

Oswald
German, meaning 'God's power'.

Otha
(alt. Otho)
German, meaning 'wealth'.

Othello
Old German, meaning 'wealth'. From the Shakespearean character.

Otis
German, meaning 'wealth'.

Otten
English, meaning 'otter-like'.

Otto
Italian, meaning 'eight'.

Ovid
Latin, meaning 'sheep'. Associated with the Roman poet.

Owain
Welsh, meaning 'youth'.

Owen
Welsh, meaning 'well born and noble'.

Oz
Hebrew, meaning 'strength'.

Palindrome names

Bob
Ebbe
Kuruk
Masam
Neven
Okko
Otto
Pip
Ramar
Uku

Boys' names

Pablo

Spanish, meaning 'little'.

Paco

Native American, meaning 'eagle'. Also a Spanish alternative for Francisco.

Padma

Indian, meaning 'lotus'.

Padraig

Irish, meaning 'noble'.

Panos

Greek, meaning 'all holy'.

Paolo

Italian, meaning 'little'.

Paresh

Indian, meaning 'supreme standard'.

Paris

From France's capital city. Also the Trojan prince in Homer's *Iliad* and Juliet's suitor in Shakespeare's *Romeo and Juliet*.

Pascal

Latin, meaning 'Easter child'.

Pat

Shortened form of Patrick, meaning 'noble'.

Patrice

Variant of Patrick, meaning 'noble'.

P

Patrick
Irish, meaning 'noble'.

Patten
English, meaning 'noble'.

Paul
Hebrew, meaning 'small'.

Pavel
Latin, meaning 'small'.

Pax
Latin, meaning 'peace'.

Paxton
English, meaning 'town of peace'.

Payne
Latin, meaning 'peasant'.

Payton
Latin, meaning 'peasant's town'.

Pedro
Spanish form of Peter, meaning 'rock'.

Penn
English, meaning 'hill'.

Percival
French, meaning 'pierce the valley'.

Percy
Shortened form of Percival, meaning 'pierce the valley'.

Perez
Hebrew, meaning 'breach'.

Pericles
Greek, meaning 'far-famed'.

Perrin
Greek, meaning 'rock'.

Perry
English, meaning 'rock'.

Pervis
English, meaning 'purveyor'.

Pesah
(alt. Pesach, Pesasch)
Hebrew, meaning 'spared'.

Pete
Shortened form of Peter, meaning 'rock'.

Peter

Greek, meaning 'rock'.

Petros

Greek form of Peter, meaning 'rock'.

Peyton

Old English, meaning 'fighting man's estate'.

Phil

Shortened form of Philip, meaning 'lover of horses'.

Philemon

Greek, meaning 'affectionate'.

Philip

Greek, meaning 'lover of horses'.

Philo

Greek, meaning 'love'.

Phineas

(alt. Pinchas)

Hebrew, meaning 'oracle'.

Phoenix

Greek, meaning 'dark red'.

Pierre

French form of Peter, meaning 'rock'.

Piers

Greek form of Peter, meaning 'rock'.

Pierson

Variant of Pierce, meaning 'son of Piers'.

Pip

Greek, shortened form of Philip, meaning 'lover of horses'.

No-nickname names

Alex
Beau
Cole
Jude
Keith
Miles
Morgan
Otto
Owen
Toby

P

Placido

Latin, meaning 'placid'.

Pradeep

Hindi, meaning 'light'.

Pranav

Hindi, meaning 'spiritual leader'.

Presley

Old English, meaning 'priest's meadow'.

Preston

Old English, meaning 'priest's town'.

Primo

Italian, meaning 'first'.

Primus

Latin, meaning 'first'.

Prince

English, from the word 'prince'.

Proctor

(alt. Prockter, Procter)

Latin, meaning 'steward'.

Popular South American names

Accius
Alban
Arrian
Coatl
Lucas
Matlal
Rafael
Tuco
Vincent
Zolin

Prospero

Latin, meaning 'prosperous'.

Pryor

English, meaning 'first'.

Ptolemy

Greek, meaning 'aggressive' or 'warlike'.

Purvis

(alt. Purves, Purviss)

French, meaning 'purveyor'.

Boys' names

Qino

Chinese, meaning 'handsome'.

Quabil

Arabic, meaning 'able'.

Quadim

Arabic, meaning 'able'.

Quadir

Arabic, meaning 'powerful'.

Quaid

Irish, meaning 'fourth'.

Qued

Native American, meaning 'weaver of a decorated robe'.

Quemby

Norse, meaning 'from the woman's estate'.

Quentin

(alt. Quinten, Quintin, Quinton, Quintus)

Latin, meaning 'fifth'.

Quillan

Gaelic, meaning 'sword'.

Quillon

Gaelic, meaning 'club'.

Quincy

Old French, meaning 'estate of the fifth son'.

Quinlan

Gaelic, meaning 'fit, shapely and strong'.

Quinn

Gaelic, meaning 'counsel'.

Quinton

English, meaning 'queen's community'.

Popular North American names

Alexander
Anthony
Daniel
Ethan
Jacob
Jayden
Joshua
Michael
Noah
William

 Boys' names

Radames

Slavic, meaning 'famous joy'.

Raekwon

Hebrew, meaning 'God has healed'.

Rafael

(alt. Rafe, Rafer, Raffi, Raphael)

Hebrew, meaning 'God has healed'. One of the archangels.

Ragnar

Old Norse, meaning 'judgement warrior'.

Raheem

Arabic, meaning 'merciful and kind'.

Rahm

Hebrew, meaning 'pleasing'.

Rahul

(alt. Raoul, Raul)

Indian, meaning 'efficient'.

Raiden

(alt. Rainen)

From the Japanese god of thunder.

Rainer

Old German, meaning 'deciding warrior'.

Raj

Indian, meaning 'king'.

Rajesh

(alt. Ramesh)

Indian, meaning 'ruler of kings'.

R

Raleigh

Old English, meaning 'deer's meadow'.

Ralph

Old English, meaning 'wolf'.

Ram

English, from the word 'ram'.

Ramiro

Germanic, meaning 'powerful in battle'.

Ramone

Spanish, meaning 'wise supporter' or 'romantic'.

Ramsey

(alt. Ramsay)

Old English, meaning 'wild garlic island'.

Randall

(alt. Randolph)

Old German, meaning 'wolf shield'.

Randy

Variant of Randall, meaning 'wolf shield'. In modern English, randy can also mean amorous.

Raniel

English, meaning 'God is my happiness'.

Ranjit

Indian, meaning 'influenced by charm'.

Rannoch

Gaelic, meaning 'fern'.

Rashad

Arabic, meaning 'good judgment'.

Rasheed

(alt. Rashid)

Indian, meaning 'rightly guided'.

Rasmus

Greek, meaning 'beloved'.

Raven

English, from the word 'raven'.

Ravi

French, meaning 'delighted'.

Rawlins

French alternative of Roland, meaning 'renowned land'.

R

Ray
English, from the word 'ray'.

Raymond
(alt. Rayner)
English, meaning 'advisor'.

Raz
Israeli, meaning 'secret' or 'mystery'.

Reagan
Irish, meaning 'little king'.

Reggie
Latin, meaning 'regal'.

Reginald
Latin, meaning 'regal'.

Regis
Shortened form of Reginald, meaning 'regal'.

Reid
Old English, meaning 'by the reeds'.

Reilly
English, meaning 'courageous'.

Remington
English, meaning 'ridge town'.

Remus
Latin, meaning 'swift'.

Rémy
French, meaning 'from Rheims'.

Ren
Shortened form of Reginald, meaning 'regal'.

Renato
Latin, meaning 'rebirth'.

Rene
French, meaning 'rebirth'.

Popular Irish names

Brian
Cian
Connor
Eoin
Finn
Kieran
Niall
Patrick
Ronan
Sean

R

Reno

Latin, meaning 'renewed'.

Reuben

Spanish, meaning 'a son'.

Reuel

Hebrew, meaning 'friend of God'.

Rex

Latin, meaning 'king'.

Rey

Spanish, meaning 'king'.

Reynold

Latin, meaning 'king's advisor'.

Rhodes

German, meaning 'where the roses grow'. Also the name of the Greek town.

Rhodri

Welsh, meaning 'ruler of the circle'.

Rhys

Welsh, meaning 'enthusiasm'.

Ricardo

Spanish form of Richard, meaning 'powerful leader'.

Richard

Old German, meaning 'powerful leader'.

Richie

Shortened form of Richard, meaning 'powerful leader'.

Rick

Shortened form of Richard, meaning 'powerful leader'.

Ricki

Shortened form of Richard, meaning 'powerful leader'.

Ricky

Shortened form of Richard, meaning 'powerful leader'.

Ridley

English, meaning 'cleared wood'.

Rigby

English, meaning 'valley of the ruler'.

R

Ringo
English, meaning 'ring'.

Rio
Spanish, meaning 'river'.

Riordan
Gaelic, meaning 'bard'.

Rishi
Variant of Richard, meaning 'powerful leader'.

Ritchie
Shortened form of Richard, meaning 'powerful leader'.

River
Latin, meaning 'river'.

Roald
Scandinavian, meaning 'ruler'.

Rob
Shortened form of Robert, meaning 'bright fame'.

Robbie
Shortened form of Robert, meaning 'bright fame'.

Robert
Old German, meaning 'bright fame'.

Roberto
Italian form of Robert, meaning 'bright fame'.

Robin
English, from the word 'robin'.

Robinson
English, meaning 'son of Robin'.

Rocco
(alt. Rocky)
Italian, meaning 'rest'.

Rockwell
English, meaning 'of the rock well'.

Rod
Short for Rhodri, Roderick and Rodney.

Roderick
German, meaning 'famous power'.

R

Rodney
Old German, meaning 'island near the clearing'.

Rodrigo
Spanish form of Roderick, meaning 'famous power'.

Roger
Old German, meaning 'spear man'.

Roland
Old German, meaning 'renowned land'.

Rolf
Old German, meaning 'wolf'.

Rollie
(alt. Rollo)

Old German, meaning 'renowned land'.

Roman
Latin, meaning 'from Rome'.

Romeo
Latin, meaning 'pilgrim to Rome'. Made famous by Shakespeare's play.

Ron
(alt. Ronnie)

Shortened form of Ronald, meaning 'mountain of strength'.

Ronald
Norse, meaning 'mountain of strength'.

Ronan
Gaelic, meaning 'little seal'.

Rory
English, meaning 'red king'.

Ross
(alt. Russ)

Scottish, meaning 'cape'.

Popular Scottish names

Alastair
Angus
Callum
Cameron
Douglas
Fraser
Hamish
Malcolm
Roderick
Stuart

Rowan

(alt. Roan)

Gaelic, meaning 'little red one'. Also reference to the rowan tree.

Roy

Gaelic, meaning 'red'.

Ruben

Hebrew, meaning 'son'.

Rudolph

Old German, meaning 'famous wolf'.

Rudy

Shortened form of Rudolph, meaning 'famous wolf'.

Rufus

Latin, meaning 'red-haired'.

Rupert

Variant of Robert, meaning 'bright fame'.

Ruslan

Russian, meaning 'like a lion'.

Russell

Old French, meaning 'little red one'.

Rusty

English, meaning 'ruddy'.

Ryan

Gaelic, meaning 'little king'.

Ryder

English, meaning 'horseman'.

Rye

English, from the word 'rye'.

Ryker

From Richard, meaning 'powerful leader'.

Rylan

English, meaning 'land where rye is grown'.

Ryley

Old English, meaning 'rye clearing'.

Ryu

Japanese, meaning 'dragon'.

 **Boys' names**

Saar

Hebrew, meaning 'tempest'.

Saber

French, meaning 'sword'.

Sagar

African, meaning 'ruler of the water'.

Sage

English, meaning 'wise'.

Sakari

Native American, meaning 'sweet'.

Salil

Indian, meaning 'from the water'.

Salim

Arabic, meaning 'secure'.

Salvador

Spanish, meaning 'saviour'.

Salvatore

Italian, meaning 'saviour'.

Nautical names

Caspian
Dylan
Merlin
Murphy
Neptune

S

Sam
(alt. Sama, Sammie, Sammy)
Hebrew, meaning 'God is heard'. Shortened form of Samuel.

Samir
Arabic, meaning 'pleasant companion'.

Samson
Hebrew, meaning 'son of Sam'.

Samuel
Hebrew, meaning 'God is heard'.

Sandeep
Indian, meaning 'lighting the way'.

Sandro
Shortened form of Alessandro, meaning 'defending men'.

Sandy
Shortened form of Alexander, meaning 'defending men'.

Sanjay
Indian, meaning 'victory'.

Santiago
Spanish, meaning 'Saint James'.

Santino
Spanish, meaning 'little Saint James'.

Santo
(alt. Santos)
Latin, meaning 'saint'.

Sascha
Shortened Russian form of Alexander, meaning 'defending men'.

Scott
(alt. Scottie)
English, meaning 'from Scotland'.

Seamus
Irish variant of James, meaning 'he who supplants'.

Sean
(alt. Shaun)
Variant of John, meaning 'God is gracious'.

Sebastian
Greek, meaning 'revered'.

S

Sébastien
French form of Sebastian, meaning 'revered'.

Sergio
Latin, meaning 'servant'.

Seth
Hebrew, meaning 'appointed'.

Severus
Latin, meaning 'severe'. Made popular by the character Severus Snape in the Harry Potter series.

Seymour
English, from Saint-Maur in northern France.

Shalen
Arabic, meaning 'tribal leader'.

Shane
Variant of Sean, meaning 'God is gracious'.

Sharif
Arabic, meaning 'honoured'.

Shea
Gaelic, meaning 'admirable'.

Shelby
Norse, meaning 'willow'.

Sherlock
English, meaning 'fair haired'.

Sherman
Old English, meaning 'shear man'.

Shmuel
Hebrew, meaning 'his name is God'.

Shola
Arabic, meaning 'energetic'.

Sid
Shortened form of Sidney, meaning 'wide meadow'.

Names of painters

Claude (Monet)
Francis (Bacon)
Leonardo (da Vinci)
Salvador (Dali)
Vincent (Van Gogh)

S

Sidney
English, meaning 'wide meadow'.

Sigmund
Old German, meaning 'victorious hand'.

Silvanus
(alt. Silvio)
Latin, meaning 'woods'.

Sim
Swahili, shortened form of Simba, meaning 'lion'.

Simba
Swahili, meaning 'lion'.

Popular Australian names

Cooper
Ethan
Jack
Joshua
Lachlan
Noah
Oliver
Riley
Thomas
William

Simon
(alt. Simeon)
Hebrew, meaning 'to hear'.

Sinbad
Persian, meaning 'Lord of Sages'. Literary merchant adventurer.

Sindri
Norse, meaning 'dwarf'.

Sipho
African, meaning 'the unknown one'.

Sire
English, from the word 'sire'.

Sirius
Hebrew, meaning 'brightest star'. Name of Harry Potter's godfather, Sirius Black.

Skipper
English, meaning 'ship captain'.

Skyler
English, meaning 'scholar'.

Solomon
Hebrew, meaning 'peace'.

S

Sonny

American English, meaning 'son'.

Soren

Scandinavian, meaning 'brightest star'.

Spencer

English, meaning 'dispenser'.

Spike

English, from the word 'spike'.

Stamos

Greek, meaning 'reasonable'.

Stan

Shortened form of Stanley, meaning 'stony meadow'.

Stanford

English, meaning 'stone ford'.

Stanley

English, meaning 'stony meadow'.

Stavros

Greek, meaning 'crowned'.

Stellan

Latin, meaning 'starred'.

Steno

German, meaning 'stone'.

Stephen

(alt. Stefan, Stefano, Steffan)

English, meaning 'crowned'.

Steven

(alt. Steve, Stevie)

English, meaning 'crowned'.

Stewart

English, meaning 'steward'.

Stoney

English, meaning 'stone like'.

Storm

English, from the word 'storm'.

Peaceful names

Glade
Manfred
Paxton
Vale
Wilfred

S

Stuart
English, meaning 'steward'.

Sven
Norse, meaning 'boy'.

Sydney
English, meaning 'wide meadow'. Also a city in Australia.

Syed
Arabic, meaning 'lucky'.

Sylvester
Latin, meaning 'wooded'.

Syon
Indian, meaning 'followed by good'.

Boys' names

Tacitus

Latin, meaning 'silent, calm'. From the Roman historian.

Tad

English, from the word 'tadpole'.

Taine

Gaelic, meaning 'river'.

Taj

Indian, meaning 'crown'.

Takashi

Japanese, meaning 'praiseworthy'.

Takoda

Sioux, meaning 'friend to everyone'.

Talbot

(alt. Tal)

English, an aristocratic name.

Tamir

Arabic, meaning 'tall and wealthy'.

Taras

(alt. Tarez)

Scottish, meaning 'crag'.

Tarek

Arabic, meaning 'evening caller'.

Tarian

Welsh, meaning 'silver'.

Tariq

Arabic, meaning 'morning star'.

T

Tarquin
Latin, from the Roman clan name.

Tarun
Hindi, meaning 'young'.

Tatanka
Hebrew, meaning 'bull'.

Tate
English, meaning 'cheerful'.

Taurean
English, meaning 'bull like'.

Tavares
English, meaning 'descendant of the hermit'.

Popular Asian names

Chang
Fang
Hiro
Hiroshi
Kane
Koji
Rei
Shin
Yemon
Zinan

Tave
(alt. Tavian, Tavis, Tavish)
French, from Gustave, meaning 'royal staff'.

Tavor
Hebrew, meaning 'misfortunate'.

Taylor
English, meaning 'tailor'.

Ted
(alt. Teddy)
English, from Edward, meaning 'wealthy guard'.

Terence
(alt. Terrill, Terry)
English, meaning 'tender'.

Tex
English, meaning 'Texan'.

Thabo
African, meaning 'filled with happiness'.

Thane
(alt. Thayer)
Scottish, meaning 'landholder'.

Thelonius
Latin, meaning 'ruler of the people'.

Theo

Shortened form of Theodore, meaning 'God's gift'.

Theodore

Greek, meaning 'God's gift'.

Theophile

Latin, meaning 'God's love'.

Theron

Greek, meaning 'hunter'.

Thierry

French variant of Terence, meaning 'tender'.

Thomas

Aramaic, meaning 'twin'.

Thomsen

English, meaning 'son of Thomas'.

Thor

Norse, meaning 'thunder'.

Tiago

From Santiago, meaning 'Saint James'.

Tibor

Latin, from the river Tiber.

Tieman

Gaelic, meaning 'lord'.

Tien

Vietnamese, meaning 'first'.

Tim

Shortened form of Timothy, meaning 'God's honour'.

Timothy

Greek, meaning 'God's honour'.

Tito

(alt. Titus)

Latin, meaning 'defender'.

Tobias

(alt. Toby)

Hebrew, meaning 'God is good'.

Tod

(alt. Todd)

English, meaning 'fox'.

Tom

(alt. Tomlin, Tommy)

Aramaic, meaning 'twin'.

Tonneau

French, meaning 'barrel'.

Tony
Shortened form of Anthony, from the old Roman family name.

Torey
Norse, meaning 'Thor'.

Torin
Gaelic, meaning 'chief'.

Torquil
Gaelic, meaning 'helmet'.

Toshi
Japanese, meaning 'reflection'.

Travis
French, meaning 'crossover'.

Trevelian
Welsh, meaning 'of the house of Eden'.

Trevor
Welsh, meaning 'great settlement'.

Trey
(alt. Tyree)
French, meaning 'very'.

Tristan
(alt. Tristram)
Celtic, from the Celtic hero.

Troy
Gaelic, meaning 'descended from the soldier'.

Tudor
Variant of Theodore, 'God's gift'.

Tyler
English, meaning 'tile maker'.

Tyrell
French, meaning 'puller'.

Tyrone
Gaelic, meaning 'Owen's county'.

Tyson
English, meaning 'son of Tyrone'.

Famous rugby players

Brian (O'Driscoll)
Gavin (Henson)
Jonny (Wilkinson)
Lawrence (Dallaglio)
Martin (Johnson)
Thom (Evans)
Toby (Flood)

 Boys' names

Uberto
(alt. Umberto)
Italian, variant of Hubert, meaning 'bright or shining intellect'.

Udath
(alt. Udathel)
Indian, meaning 'noble'.

Udo
German, meaning 'power of the wolf'.

Ugo
Italian form of Hugo, meaning 'mind and heart'.

Ulf
German, meaning 'wolf'.

Ulrich
German, meaning 'noble ruler'.

Ultan
Irish, meaning 'from Ulster'.

Ulysses
Greek, meaning 'wrathful'. Made famous by the mythological voyager.

Unwyn
(alt. Unwin, Unwine)
English, meaning 'unfriendly'.

Upton
English, meaning 'high town'.

Urho
Finnish, meaning 'brave'.

Uri

(alt. Uriah, Urias)

Hebrew, meaning 'my light'.

Uriel

Hebrew, meaning 'angel of light'. One of the archangels.

Usher

English, from the word 'usher'. Made famous by the American R&B star.

Uttam

Indian, meaning 'best'.

Uzi

Hebrew, meaning 'my strength'.

Uzzi

(alt. Uzziah)

Hebrew, meaning 'my power'.

Christmas names

Christian
Ebenezer
Gabriel
Joseph
Nicholas
Noel
Wenceslas

Boys' names

Vaclav

Czech, meaning 'receives glory'.

Vadim

Russian, meaning 'scandal maker'.

Valdemar

German, meaning 'renowned leader'.

Valente

Latin, meaning 'valiant'.

Valentin
(alt. Val)

French, meaning 'valentine'.

Valentine

English, from the word 'valentine'.

Valentino

Italian, meaning 'valentine'.

Valerio

Italian, meaning 'valiant'.

Valia

Indian, meaning 'king of the monkeys'.

Van

Dutch, meaning 'son of'.

Vance

English, meaning 'marshland'.

V

Vangelis
Greek, meaning 'good news'.

Varro
Latin, meaning 'strong'.

Varun
Hindi, meaning 'water god'.

Vasilis
Greek, meaning 'kingly'.

Vaughan
Welsh, meaning 'little'.

Vernell
French, meaning 'green and flourishing'.

Verner
German, meaning 'army defender'.

Vernon
(alt. Vernie)
French, meaning 'alder grove'.

Versilius
Latin, meaning 'flier'.

Vester
Latin, meaning 'wooded'.

Vibol
Cambodian, meaning 'man of plenty'.

Shakespearean names

Angelo *(Measure for Measure)*
Anthony *(Anthony and Cleopatra)*
Balthazar *(Romeo and Juliet)*
Hamlet *(Hamlet)*
Henry *(Henry V)*
Iago *(Othello)*
Othello *(Othello)*
Richard *(Richard III)*
Romeo *(Romeo and Juliet)*
Sebastian *(Twelfth Night)*

Victor
Latin, meaning 'champion'.

Vidal
(alt. Vidar)
Spanish, meaning 'life giving'.

Vijay
Hindi, meaning 'conquering'.

Vikram
Hindi, meaning 'sun'.

Viktor
Latin, meaning 'victory'.

Ville
French, meaning 'town'.

Vincent
(alt. Vince)
English, meaning 'victorious'.

Virgil
Latin, meaning 'staff bearer'.
From the Latin poet.

Vito
Spanish, meaning 'life'.

Vittorio
Italian, meaning 'victory'.

Vitus
Latin, meaning 'life'.

Vivek
Indian, meaning 'wisdom'.

Vivian
Latin, meaning 'lively'.

Vladimir
Slavic, meaning 'prince'.

Volker
German, meaning 'defender of the people'.

Von
Norse, meaning 'hope'.

 **Boys' names**

Wade

English, meaning 'to move forward' or 'to go'.

Waldemar

German, meaning 'famous ruler'.

Walden

English, meaning 'valley of the Britons'.

Waldo

Old German, meaning 'rule'.

Walker

English, meaning 'a fuller'.

Wallace

English, meaning 'foreigner' or 'stranger'.

Wally

German, meaning 'ruler of the army'.

Walter

(alt. Walt)

German, meaning 'ruler of the army'.

Wasim

Arabic, meaning 'attractive' or 'full of grace'.

Ward

English, meaning 'guardian'.

Wardell

Old English, meaning 'watchman's hill'.

Warner

German, meaning 'army guard'.

Warren

German, meaning 'guard' or 'the game park'.

Warwick

English, meaning 'farm near the weir'.

Washington

English, meaning 'clever' or 'clever man's settlement'.

Wassily

Greek, meaning 'royal' or 'kingly'.

Watson

English, meaning 'son' or 'son of Walter'.

Waverley

(alt. Waverly)

English, meaning 'quaking aspen'.

Waylon

English, meaning 'land by the road'.

Wayne

English, meaning 'a cartwright'.

Webster

English, meaning 'weaver'.

Weldon

English, meaning 'from the hill of well' or 'hill with a well'.

Wendell

(alt. Wendel)

German, meaning 'a wend'.

Werner

German, meaning 'army guard'.

Werther

German, meaning 'a soldier in the army'.

Weston

English, meaning 'from the west town'.

Wheeler

English, meaning 'wheel maker'.

Whitley

English, meaning 'white wood'.

Whitman

Old English, meaning 'white man'.

Whitney

Old English, meaning 'white island'.

Wilber
(alt. Wilbur)

Old German, meaning 'bright will'.

Wildon

English, meaning 'wooded hill'.

Wiley

Old English, meaning 'beguiling' or 'enchanting'.

Wilford

Old English, meaning 'the ford by the willows'.

Wilfredo
(alt. Wilfred, Wilfrid)

English, meaning 'to will peace'.

Wilhelm

German, meaning 'strong-willed warrior'.

Wilkes
(alt. Wilkie)

Old English, meaning 'strong-willed protector' or 'strong and resolute protector'.

William
(alt. Will, Willie)

English (Teutonic), meaning 'strong protector' or 'strong-willed warrior'.

Willis

English, meaning 'server of William'.

Willoughby

Old Norse and Old English, meaning 'from the farm by the trees'.

Wilmer

English (Teutonic), meaning 'famously resolute'.

Wilmot

English, meaning 'resolute mind'.

Wilson

English, meaning 'son of William'.

Wilton

Old Norse and English, meaning 'from the farm by the brook' or 'from the farm by the streams'.

Windell
(alt. Wendell)

German, meaning 'wanderer' or 'seeker'.

Windsor

Old English, meaning 'river bank' or 'landing place'.

Winfield

English, meaning 'from the field of Wina'.

Winslow

Old English, meaning 'victory on the hill'.

Winter

Old English, meaning 'to be born in the winter'.

Winthrop

Old English, meaning 'village of friends'.

Knights of the round table

Arthur
Gareth
Gawain
Lancelot
Tristram

Winton

Old English, meaning 'a friend's farm'.

Wirrin

Aboriginal, meaning 'a tea tree'.

Wistan

Old English, meaning 'battle stone' or 'mark of the battle'.

Wittan

Old English, meaning 'farm in the woods' or 'farm by the woods'.

Wolf
(alt. Wolfe)

English, meaning 'strong as a wolf'.

Wolfgang

Teutonic, meaning 'the path of wolves'.

Wolfrom

Teutonic, meaning 'raven wolf'.

Wolter

Dutch, a form of Walter meaning 'ruler of the army'.

Woodburn

Old English, meaning 'a stream in the woods'.

Woodrow

English, meaning 'from the row of houses by the wood'.

Woodward

English, meaning 'guardian of the forest'.

Woody

American, meaning 'path in the woods'.

Worcester

Old English, meaning 'from a Roman site'.

Worth

American, meaning 'worth much' or 'wealthy place' or 'wealth and riches'.

Wren

Old English, meaning 'tiny bird'.

Wright

Old English, meaning 'to be a craftsman' or 'from a carpenter'.

Wyatt

Teutonic, meaning 'from wood' or 'from the wide water'.

Wyclef

(alt. Wycleff, Wycliff, Wycliffe)

English, meaning 'inhabitant of the white cliff'.

Wynn

(alt. Wyn)

Welsh, meaning 'very blessed' or 'the fair blessed one'.

Popular Welsh names

Aeron	Gareth
Aled	Gwyn
Bryn	Owain
Dylan	Rhys
Evan	Wallace

X

Boys' names

Xadrian

American, a combination of X and Adrian, meaning 'from Hadria'.

Xander

Greek, meaning 'defender of the people'.

Xannon

American, meaning 'descendant of an ancient family'.

Xanthus

Greek, meaning 'golden-haired'.

Xavier

Latin, meaning 'to the new house'.

Xenon

Greek, meaning 'the guest'.

Xerxes

Persian, meaning 'ruler of the people' or 'respected king'.

Xeven

Slavic, meaning 'lively'.

Xylander

Greek, meaning 'man of the forest'.

Bird names

Gannet
Phoenix
Robin
Tern
Wren

Boys' names

Yaal

Hebrew, meaning 'ascending' or 'one to ascend'.

Yadid

Hebrew, meaning 'the beloved one'.

Yadon

Hebrew, meaning 'against judgment'.

Yahir

Spanish, meaning 'handsome one'.

Yaholo

Native American, meaning 'yells'.

Yair

Hebrew, meaning 'the enlightening one' or 'illuminating'.

Yakiya

Hebrew, meaning 'pure' or 'bright'.

Yanis
(alt. Yannis)

Greek, a form of John meaning 'gift of God'.

Yarden

Hebrew, meaning 'to flow downward'.

Ye

Chinese, meaning 'bright one' or 'light'.

Yehuda

Hebrew, meaning 'to praise and exalt'.

Yered

Hebrew, a form of Jared, meaning 'descending'.

Yerik

Russian, meaning 'God-appointed one'.

Yerodin

African, meaning 'studious'.

Yervant

Armenian, meaning 'king of people'.

Yitzak

(alt. Yitzaak)

Hebrew, meaning 'laughter' or 'one who laughs'.

Ynyr

Welsh, meaning 'to honour'.

Yobachi

African, meaning 'one who prays to God' or 'prayed to God'.

Yogi

Japanese, meaning 'one who practises yoga' or 'from yoga'.

Yoloti

Aztec, meaning 'heart'.

Yona

Native American, meaning 'bear'; and also Hebrew, meaning 'dove'.

York

Celtic, meaning 'yew tree' or 'from the farm of the yew tree'.

Yosef

Hebrew, meaning 'added by God' or 'God shall add'.

Yuri

Aboriginal, meaning 'to hear'; Japanese, meaning 'one to listen'; Russian, a form of George meaning 'farmer'.

Yuuta

Japanese, meaning 'excellent'.

Yves

French, meaning 'miniature archer' or 'small archer'.

Z Boys' names

Zachariah
(alt. Zac, Zach, Zachary)
Hebrew, meaning 'remembered
by the Lord' or 'God has
remembered'.

Zad
Persian, meaning 'my son'.

Zada
(alt. Zadan, Zadin, Zadun)
Dutch, meaning 'a man who
sowed seeds'.

Zadok
Hebrew, meaning 'righteous
one'.

Zador
Hungarian, meaning 'violent
demeanour'.

Zafar
Arabic, meaning 'triumphant'.

Zaid
African, meaning 'increase the
growth' or 'growth'.

Popular Spanish names

Alejandro
Carlos
Diego
Ivan
Javier
Jorge
Marcos
Mario
Pablo
Raul

Zaide

Yiddish, meaning 'the elder ones'.

Zain

(alt. Zane)

Arabic, meaning 'the handsome son'.

Zaire

African, meaning 'river from Zaire'.

Zander

Greek, meaning 'defender of my people'.

Zarek

Persian, meaning 'God protect our King'.

Zoltan

(alt. Zoltin)

Hungarian, meaning 'life'.

Fiery names

Aidan
Blaze
Flint
Kenneth

part three

Girls' Names

 Girls' names

A'mari

Variation of the Swahili or Muslim name Amira, meaning 'princess'.

Aanya

Variation of the Russian name Anya, meaning 'favour' or 'grace'. Also Sanskrit, meaning 'the inexhaustible'.

Aaryanna

Derivative of the Latin and Greek name Ariadne, both meaning 'the very holy one'.

Abby
(alt. Abbey, Abbie)

Form of Abigail, Hebrew, meaning 'my father's joy'.

Abigail
(alt. Abagail, Abbiegayle, Abbigail, Abigale, Abigayle)

Hebrew, meaning 'my father's joy'.

Abilene
(alt. Abilee)

Latin and Spanish for 'hazelnut'.

Abina
(alt. Abena)

Ghanaian, meaning 'born on Tuesday'.

Abra

Female variation of Abraham. Also Sanskrit, meaning 'clouds'.

Abril

Spanish for the month of April. Also Latin, meaning 'open'.

Acacia

Greek, meaning 'point' or 'thorn'. Also a species of flowering trees and shrubs.

Acadia

Variation of the Greek word arcadia meaning 'paradise'. Originally, a French colony in Canada.

Ada

(alt. Adair)

Hebrew, meaning 'adornment'.

Adalee

German, meaning 'noble'.

Adalia

Hebrew, meaning 'God is my refuge'.

Addie

(alt. Addy, Adi)

Shortened form of Addison, Adelaide, Adele and Adeline.

Addison

(alt. Addisyn, Addyson)

English, meaning 'son of Adam'.

Adelaide

(alt. Adelaida)

German, popular after the rule of William IV and Queen Adelaide of England in the 19th century.

Adele

(alt. Adela, Adelia, Adell, Adella, Adelle)

German, meaning 'noble' or 'nobility'.

Adeline

(alt. Adalyn, Adalynn, Adelina, Adelyn)

Variant of Adelaide, meaning 'noble'.

Aden

(alt. Addien)

Hebrew, meaning 'decoration'.

Adeola

(alt. Adeolah, Adeolla)

African, meaning 'weaver of a crown of honour'.

Aderyn

Welsh, meaning 'bird'.

A

Adesina

Nigerian, meaning 'she paves the way'. Usually given to a firstborn daughter.

Adia

Variant of Ada, meaning 'adornment'.

Adina

(alt. Adena)

Hebrew, meaning 'high hopes' or 'precious'.

Adira

Hebrew, meaning 'noble' or 'powerful'.

Adrian

Italian, from the northern city of Hadria.

Adrianna

(alt. Adriana)

Variant of Adrienne, meaning 'rich' or 'dark'.

Adrienne

(alt. Adriane, Adrianne)

Greek, meaning 'rich', or Latin, meaning 'dark'.

Aegle

Greek, meaning 'brightness' or 'splendour'.

Movie inspirations

Bridget (*Bridget Jones's Diary*)
Cady (*Mean Girls*)
Fiona (*Shrek*)
Holly (*Breakfast at Tiffany's*)
Isabella, Bella (*Twilight*)
Lara (*Tomb Raider*)
Maria (*The Sound of Music*)
Marla (*Fight Club*)
Mary (*Mary Poppins*)
Nina (*Black Swan*)
Pandora (*Avatar*)
Trinity (*The Matrix*)

Aerin

Variant of Erin, meaning 'peace-making'.

Aerith

American, from a character in the computer game *Final Fantasy VII*.

Aero
(alt. Aeron)

Greek, meaning 'water'.

Aerolynn

Combination of the Greek Aero, meaning 'water', and the English Lynn, meaning 'waterfall'.

Afia
(alt. Aff, Affi)

Arabic, meaning 'a child born on Friday'.

Africa

Celtic, meaning 'pleasant', as well as the name of the continent.

Afsaneh

Iranian, meaning 'a fairy tale'.

Afsha

Persian, meaning 'one who sprinkles light'.

Afton

Originally a place name in Scotland.

Agatha

From Saint Agatha, the patron saint of bells, meaning 'good'.

Aglaia

One of the three Greek Graces, meaning 'brilliance'.

Agnes

Greek, meaning 'virginal' or 'pure'.

Agrippina

Latin, from the expression, meaning 'born feet first'.

Aida

Arabic, meaning 'reward' or 'present'.

Aidanne
(alt. Aidan, Aidenn)

Gaelic, meaning 'fire'.

Ailbhe

Irish, meaning 'noble' or 'bright'.

Aileen
(alt. *Aelinn, Aleen, Aline, Alline, Eileen*)

Gaelic variant of Helen, meaning 'light'.

Ailith
(alt. *Ailish*)

Old English, meaning 'seasoned warrior'.

Ailsa
Scottish, meaning 'pledge from God', as well as the name of a Scottish island, Ailsa Craig.

Aimee
(alt. *Aimie, Amie*)

French form of Amy, meaning 'beloved'.

Aina
Scandinavian, meaning 'forever'.

Aine
(alt. *Aino*)

Celtic, meaning 'happiness'.

Ainsley
Scottish and Gaelic, meaning 'one's own meadow'.

Aisha
(alt. *Aeysha*)

Arabic, meaning 'woman'; as well as Swahili, meaning 'life'.

Aishwarya
Variant of the Arabic Aisha, meaning 'woman'.

Aislinn
(alt. *Aislin, Aisling, Aislyn, Alene, Allene*)

Irish Gaelic, meaning 'dream'.

Aiyanna
(alt. *Aiyana*)

Native American, meaning 'forever flowering'.

Aja
Hindi, meaning 'goat'.

Aka
(alt. *Akah, Akkah*)

Maori, meaning 'loving one'.

Akela
(alt. *Akilah*)

Hawaiian, meaning 'noble'.

Akilina
Greek or Russian, meaning 'eagle'.

Akiva

Hebrew, meaning 'protect and shelter'.

Alaina

(alt. Alane, Alani, Alayna, Aleena)

Feminine of Alan, from the Gaelic for 'rock' or 'comely'.

Alana

(alt. Alanna, Alannah)

Variant of Alaina, meaning 'rock' or 'comely'.

Alanis

(alt. Alarice)

Variant of Alaina, meaning 'rock' or 'comely'.

Alba

Latin, meaning 'white'. Also the Gaelic word for 'Scotland'.

Alberta

(alt. Albertha, Albertine)

Feminine of Albert, from the Old German for 'noble, bright, famous'.

Albina

Latin, meaning 'white' or 'fair'.

Alda

German, meaning 'old' or 'prosperous'.

Aldis

English, meaning 'battle-seasoned'.

Aleah

Arabic, meaning 'high'; also Persian, meaning 'one of God's beings'.

Aleta

(alt. Aletha)

Greek, meaning 'footloose'.

Alethea

(alt. Aletheia)

Greek, meaning 'truth'.

Alex

(alt. Alexa, Alexi, Alexia, Alexina)

Shortened version of Alexandra, meaning 'man's defender'.

Alexandra

(alt. Alejandra, Alejhandra, Aleksandra, Alessandra, Alexandria)

Feminine of Alexander, from the Greek interpretation of 'man's defender'.

A

Alexis
(alt. Alexus, Alexys)
Greek, meaning 'helper'.

Aleydis
Variant of Alice, meaning 'noble' or 'nobility'.

Alfreda
Old English, meaning 'elf power'.

Ali
(alt. Allie, Ally)
Shortened version of Alexandra, Aliyah or Alice.

Alibeth
Variant of Elizabeth, meaning 'consecrated to God'.

Alice
(alt. Alize, Alyce, Alys, Alyse)
English, meaning 'noble' or 'nobility'.

Alicia
(alt. Ahlicia, Alecia, Alesia, Alessia, Alizia, Alycia, Alysia)
Variant of Alice, meaning 'nobility'.

Alida
(alt. Aleida)
Latin, meaning 'small winged one'.

Alienor
(alt. Aliana)
Variant of Eleanor, from the Greek for 'light'.

Aliki
(alt. Alika)
Variant of Alice, meaning 'nobility'.

Alima
Arabic, meaning 'cultured'.

Alina
(alt. Alena)
Slavic variation of Helen, meaning 'light'.

Alisha
(alt. Alesha, Alysha)
Variant of Alice, meaning 'nobility'.

Alison
(alt. Allison, Allisyn, Allyson, Alyson)
Variant of Alice, meaning 'nobility'.

Alissa
(alt. Alessa, Alise)

Greek, meaning 'pretty'.

Alivia

Variant of Olivia, meaning 'olive tree'.

Aliya
(alt. Aaliyah, Aleah, Alia, Aliah, Aliyah)

Arabic, meaning 'exalted' or 'sublime'.

Alla

Variant of Ella or Alexandra. Also a possible reference to Allah.

Allegra

Italian, meaning 'joyous'.

Allura

French, from the word for entice, meaning 'the power of attraction'.

Allyn

Feminine of Alan, meaning 'peaceful'.

Alma

Three possible origins: Latin for 'giving nurture', Italian for 'soul' and Arabic for 'learned'.

Almeda
(alt. Almeta)

Latin, meaning 'ambitious'.

Almera
(alt. Almira)

Feminine of Elmer, from the Arabic for 'aristocratic' and the Old English meaning 'noble'.

Alohi

Variant of the Hawaiian greeting Aloha, meaning 'love and affection'.

Alona

Hebrew, meaning 'oak tree'.

Alora

Variant of Alona, meaning 'oak tree'.

Alpha

The first letter of the Greek alphabet, usually given to a firstborn daughter.

Alta

Latin, meaning 'elevated'.

Altagracia

Spanish, meaning 'grace'.

Althea

(alt. Altea, Altha)

Greek, meaning 'healing power'.

Alva

Spanish, meaning 'blonde' or 'fair skinned'.

Alvena

(alt. Alvina)

English, meaning 'noble friend'.

Alvia

(alt. Alyvia)

Variant of Olivia, meaning 'olive tree' or Elvira from the ancient Spanish city.

Alyssa

(alt. Alisa, Allyssa, Alysa)

Greek, meaning 'rational'.

Amabel

Variant of Annabel, meaning 'grace and beauty'.

Amadea

Feminine of Amadeus, meaning 'God's'.

Amalia

Variant of Emilia, Latin, meaning 'rival, eager'.

Amana

Hebrew, meaning 'loyal and true'.

Amanda

Latin, meaning 'much loved'.

Amandine

Variant of Amanda, meaning 'much loved'.

Amara

(alt. Amani)

Greek, meaning 'lovely forever'.

Amarantha

Contraction of Amanda and Samantha, meaning 'much loved listener'.

Amaris

(alt. Amari, Amasa, Amata, Amaya)

Hebrew, meaning 'pledged by God'.

Amaryllis

Greek, meaning 'fresh'. Also a flower by the same name.

Amber

French, from the word for the semi-precious stone of the same name.

Amberly

Contraction of Amber and Leigh, meaning 'stone' and 'meadow'.

Amberlynn

Contraction of Amber and Lynn, meaning 'stone' and 'waterfall'.

Amboree

(alt. Amber, Ambree)

American, meaning 'precocious'.

Amelia

(alt. Aemilia)

Greek, meaning 'industrious'.

Amelie

(alt. Amalie)

French form of Amelia, meaning 'industrious'.

America

From the country of the same name.

Ameris

Variant of Amaryllis, meaning 'fresh'.

Amethyst

Greek, from the word for the precious, mulberry coloured stone of the same name.

Amina

Arabic, meaning 'honest and trustworthy'.

Amira

(alt. Amiya, Amiyah)

Arabic, meaning 'a high-born girl'.

Amity

Latin, meaning 'friendship and harmony'.

Amory

Variant of the Spanish name Amor, meaning 'love'.

Amy

(alt. Amee, Ami, Amie, Ammie)

Latin, meaning 'beloved'.

Amya

Variant of Amy, meaning 'beloved'.

Ana-Lisa

Contraction of Anna and Lisa, meaning 'grace' or 'consecrated to God'.

Anafa

Hebrew, meaning 'heron'.

Ananda

Hindi, meaning 'bliss'.

Anastasia

(alt. Athanasia)

Greek, meaning 'resurrection'.

Anatolia

From the eastern Greek town of the same name.

Andelyn

Contraction of the feminine for Andrew and Lynn, meaning 'strong waterfall'.

Andrea

(alt. Andreia, Andria)

Feminine of Andrew, from the Greek term for 'a man's woman'.

Andrine

Variant of Andrea, meaning 'a man's woman'.

Andromeda

Greek, meaning 'leader of men'. From the heroine of a Greek legend.

Anemone

Greek, meaning 'breath'. Also from the flower.

Angela

(alt. Angel, Angeles, Angelia Angelle, Angie)

Greek, meaning 'messenger from God' or 'angel'.

Angelica

(alt. Angelina, Angeline, Angelique, Angelise, Angelita, Anjelica)

Latin, meaning 'angelic'.

Anise

(alt. Anisa, Anissa)

French, from the licorice flavoured plant of the same name.

Anita

(alt. Anitra)

Variant of Ann, meaning 'grace'.

Ann

(alt. Anne, Annie)

Derived from Hannah, meaning 'grace'.

229

Anna
(alt. Ana, Anne)
Derived from Hannah, meaning 'grace'.

Annabel
(alt. Anabel, Anabelle, Annabell, Annabella, Annabelle)
Contraction of Anna and Belle, meaning 'grace' and 'beauty'.

Annalise
(alt. Annalee, Annaliese, Annalisa, Anneli, Annelie, Annelies, Annelise)
Contraction of Anna and Lise, meaning 'grace' and 'pledged to God'.

Annemarie
(alt. Annamae, Annamarie, Annelle, Annmarie)
Contraction of Anna and Mary, meaning 'grace' and 'star of the sea'.

Annette
(alt. Annetta)
Derived from Hannah, Hebrew, meaning 'grace'.

Annis
Greek, meaning 'finished or completed'.

Annora
Latin, meaning 'honour'.

Anoushka
(alt. Anousha)
Russian variant of Ann, meaning 'grace'.

Ansley
English, meaning 'the awesome one's meadow'.

Anthea
(alt. Anthi)
Greek, meaning 'flowerlike'.

Antigone
In Greek mythology, Antigone was the daughter of Oedipus.

Antoinette
(alt. Anonetta, Antonette, Antonietta)
Both a variation of Ann and the feminine of Anthony, meaning 'invaluable grace'.

Antonia
(alt. Antonella, Antonina)
Latin, meaning 'invaluable'.

Anwen
Welsh, meaning 'very fair'.

A

Anya
(alt. Aniya, Aniyah, Aniylah, Anja)
Russian, meaning 'grace'.

Aoife
Gaelic, meaning 'beautiful joy'.

Apollonia
Feminine of Apollo, the Greek god of the sun.

Apple
From the name of the fruit.

April
(alt. Avril)
Latin, meaning 'opening up'. Also the name of the month.

Aquilina
(alt. Aqua, Aquila)
Spanish, meaning 'like an eagle'.

Ara
Arabic, meaning 'brings rain'.

Arabella
Latin, meaning 'answered prayer'.

Araceli
(alt. Aracely)
Spanish, meaning 'altar of Heaven'.

Araylia
(alt. Araelea)
Latin, meaning 'golden'.

Arcadia
Greek, meaning 'paradise'.

Ardelle
(alt. Ardell, Ardella)
Latin, meaning 'burning with enthusiasm'.

Arden
(alt. Ardis, Ardith)
Latin, meaning 'burning with enthusiasm'.

Arella
(alt. Areli, Arely)
Hebrew, meaning 'angel'.

Aretha
Greek, meaning 'woman of virtue'.

Aria
(alt. Ariah)
Italian, meaning 'melody'.

Ariadne

Greek and Latin, meaning 'the very holy one'. In Greek mythology, Ariadne was the daughter of King Minos.

Ariana

(alt. Ariane, Arianna, Arienne)

Welsh, meaning 'silver'.

Ariel

(alt. Ariela, Ariella, Arielle)

Hebrew, meaning 'lioness of God'. One of the archangels.

Arlene

(alt. Arleen, Arlie, Arline, Arly)

Gaelic, meaning 'pledge'.

Armida

Latin, meaning 'little armed one'.

Artemisia

(alt. Artemis)

Greek and Spanish, meaning 'perfect'.

Artie

(alt. Arti)

Shortened form of Artemisia, meaning 'perfect'.

Ashanti

From the geographical area in Ghana, Africa.

Ashby

English, meaning 'ash tree farm'. Also name of place in Leicestershire.

Ashley

(alt. Ashely, Ashlee, Ashleigh, Ashli, Ashlie, Ashly)

English, meaning 'ash tree meadow'.

Ashlynn

(alt. Ashlyn)

Irish Gaelic, meaning 'dream'.

Ashton

(alt. Ashtyn)

Old English, meaning 'ash tree town'. From the place name.

Asia

From the name of the continent.

Asma

(alt. Asmara)

Arabic, meaning 'high-standing'.

A

Aspen
(alt. Aspynn)

From the name of the tree. Also name of a city in the USA.

Assumpta
(alt. Assunta)

Italian, meaning 'raised up'.

Asta
(alt. Asteria, Astor, Astoria)

Greek or Latin, meaning 'star-like'.

Astrid

Old Norse, meaning 'beautiful like a God'.

Atara

Hebrew, meaning 'diadem'.

Athena
(alt. Athenais)

Greek, meaning 'wise'. From the Greek goddess of wisdom.

Aubrey
(alt. Aubree, Aubriana, Aubrie)

French, meaning 'elf ruler'.

Audrey
(alt. Audra, Audrie, Audrina, Audry, Autry)

English, meaning 'noble strength'.

Audrina

Variant of Audrey, meaning 'noble strength'.

Augusta
(alt. August, Augustine)

Latin, meaning 'worthy of respect'.

Aura
(alt. Aurea)

Greek or Latin, meaning either 'soft breeze' or 'gold'.

Popular French names

Adele	Giselle
Amelie	Monique
Belle	Paulette
Colette	Sabine
Fleur	Yvette

Aurelia
(alt. Aurelie)
Latin, meaning 'gold'.

Aurora
(alt. Aurore)
Latin, meaning 'dawn'. In Roman mythology, Aurora was the goddess of sunrise.

Austine
(alt. Austen, Austin)
Latin, meaning 'worthy of respect'.

Autumn
From the name of the season

Ava
(alt. Avia, Avie)
Latin, meaning 'like a bird'.

Avalon
(alt. Avalyn, Aveline)
Celtic, meaning 'island of apples'.

Axelle
Greek, meaning 'father of peace'.

Aya
(alt. Ayah)
Hebrew, meaning 'bird'.

Ayanna
(alt. Ayana)
American, meaning 'grace'.

Ayesha
(alt. Aisha, Aysha)
Persian, meaning 'small one'.

Azalea
Latin, meaning 'dry earth'.

Azalia
Hebrew, meaning 'aided by God'.

Aziza
Hebrew, meaning 'mighty', or Arabic, meaning 'precious'.

Azure
(alt. Azaria)
French, meaning 'sky-blue'.

 Girls' names

Babette

French version of Barbara, from the Greek word meaning 'foreign'.

Badia

(alt. Badiyn, Badea)

Arabic, meaning 'elegant'.

Bailey

(alt. Baeli, Bailee)

English, meaning 'law enforcer'.

Bambi

Shortened version of the Italian Bambina, meaning 'child'.

Barbara

(alt. Barb, Barbie, Barbra)

Greek, meaning 'foreign'.

Basma

Arabic, meaning 'smile'.

Bathsheba

Hebrew, meaning 'daughter of the oath'.

Bay

(alt. Baya)

From the plant or geographical name.

Beata

Latin, meaning 'blessed'.

Beatrice

(alt. Beatrix, Beatriz, Bellatrix, Betrys)

Latin, meaning 'bringer of gladness'.

Literary names

Alice (*Alice in Wonderland*, Lewis Carroll)
Bella (Twilight novels, Stephenie Meyer)
Charlotte (*The Sorrows of Young Werther*, J. W. von Goethe)
Emma (*Madame Bovary*, Gustave Flaubert)
Esther (*Bleak House*, Charles Dickens)
Iris (*The Blind Assassin*, Margaret Atwood)
Hermione (Harry Potter series, J. K. Rowling)
Lyra (*His Dark Materials*, Phillip Pullman)
Matilda (*Matilda*, Roald Dahl)
Shirley (*Shirley*, Charlotte Brontë)
Wendy (*Peter Pan*, J. M. Barrie)

Becky
(alt. Beccie, Beccy, Beckie)

Shortened form of Rebecca, Hebrew meaning 'joined'.

Bee

Shortened form of Beatrice, meaning 'bringer of gladness'.

Belinda
(alt. Belen, Belina)

Contraction of Belle and Linda, meaning 'beautiful'.

Bell

Shortened form of Isabel, meaning 'pledged to God'.

Bella

Latin, meaning 'beautiful'.

Belle

French, meaning 'beautiful'.

Belva

Latin, meaning 'beautiful view'.

Bénédicta

Latin, the feminine of Benedict, meaning 'blessed'.

Benita
(alt. Bernita)

Spanish, meaning 'blessed'.

Bennie

Shortened version of Bénédicta and Benita, meaning 'blessed'.

Berit

(alt. Beret)

Scandinavian, meaning 'splendid' or 'gorgeous'.

Bernadette

French, meaning 'courageous'.

Bernadine

French, meaning 'courageous'.

Bernice

(alt. Berenice, Berniece, Burnice)

Greek, meaning 'she who brings victory'.

Bertha

(alt. Berta, Berthe, Bertie)

German, meaning 'bright'.

Beryl

Greek, meaning 'pale green gemstone'.

Bess

(alt. Bessie)

Shortened form of Elizabeth, meaning 'consecrated to God'.

Beth

Hebrew, meaning 'house'. Also shortened form of Elizabeth, meaning 'consecrated to God'.

Bethany

(alt. Bethan)

Hebrew, referring to a geographical location.

Bethel

Hebrew, meaning 'house of God'.

Bettina

Spanish version of Elizabeth, meaning 'consecrated to God'.

Betty

(alt. Betsy, Bette, Bettie, Bettye)

Shortened version of Elizabeth, meaning 'consecrated to God'.

Beulah

Hebrew, meaning 'married'.

Beverly

(alt. Beverlee, Beverley)

English, meaning 'beaver stream'.

Bevin

Celtic, meaning 'fair lady'.

237

Beyoncé

American, made popular by the singer.

Bianca

(alt. Blanca)

Italian, meaning 'white'.

Bibiana

Greek, meaning 'alive'.

Bijou

French, meaning 'jewel'.

Billie

(alt. Bill, Billy, Billye)

Shortened version of Wilhelmina, meaning 'determined'.

Bina

Hebrew, meaning 'knowledge'.

Birgit

(alt. Birgitta)

Norwegian, meaning 'splendid'.

Blair

Scottish Gaelic, meaning 'flat, plain area'.

Blake

(alt. Blakely, Blakelyn)

English, meaning either 'pale-skinned' or 'dark'.

Blanche

(alt. Blanch)

French, meaning 'white or pale'.

Bliss

English, meaning 'intense happiness'.

Blithe

English, meaning 'joyous'.

Blodwen

Welsh, meaning 'white flower'.

Blossom

English, meaning 'flowerlike'.

Blythe

(alt. Bly)

English, meaning 'happy and carefree'.

Bobbi

(alt. Bobbie, Bobby)

Shortened version of Roberta, meaning 'bright fame'.

B

Bonamy
(alt. Bomani, Bonamia, Bonamea)

French, meaning 'close friend'.

Bonita
Spanish, meaning 'pretty'.

Bonnie
(alt. Bonny)

Scottish, meaning 'fair of face'.

Brandy
(alt. Brandee, Brandi, Brandie)

From the name of the liquor.

Branwen
Welsh, meaning 'a white crow'.

Brea
(alt. Bree, Bria)

Shortened form of Brianna, meaning 'strong'.

Brenda
Old Norse, meaning 'sword'.

Brianna
(alt. Breana, Breanna, Breanne)

Irish Gaelic, meaning 'strong'.

Bridget
(alt. Bridgett, Bridgette, Brigette, Brigid, Brigitta, Brigitte)

Irish Gaelic, meaning 'strength and power'.

Brier
French, meaning 'heather'.

Brit
(alt. Britt, Britta)

Celtic, meaning 'spotted' or 'freckled'.

Britannia
Latin, meaning 'Britain'.

Biblical names

Abigail
Delilah
Eve
Hannah
Mary
Naomi
Rebecca
Ruth
Sarah
Salome

Brittany
(alt. Britany, Britney, Britni, Brittani, Brittanie, Brittney, Brittni, Brittny)

Latin, meaning 'from England'.

Bronwyn
(alt. Bronwen)

Welsh, meaning 'fair breast'.

Brooke
(alt. Brook)

English, meaning 'small stream'.

Brooklyn
(alt. Brooklynn)

From the name of a New York borough.

Brunhilda

German, meaning 'armour-wearing fighting maid'.

Bryn
(alt. Brynn)

Welsh, meaning 'mount'.

Bryony
(alt. Briony)

From the name of a European vine.

Buffy

American alternative of Elizabeth, meaning 'consecrated to God'.

Popular Spanish names

Ana
Carla
Carmen
Daniela
Elena
Maria
Marina
Natalia
Sara
Sofia

B

 Girls' names

Cadence
Latin, meaning 'with rhythm'.

Cadew
French, meaning 'gift'.

Cai
Vietnamese, meaning 'feminine'.

Caitlin
(alt. Cadyn, Caitlann, Caitlyn, Caitlynn)
Greek, meaning 'pure'.

Calandra
Greek, meaning 'lark'.

Calantha
(alt. Calanthe)
Greek, meaning 'lovely flower'.

Caledonia
Latin, meaning 'from Scotland'.

Calia
American, meaning 'renowned beauty'.

Calla
Greek, meaning 'beautiful'.

Callie
(alt. Caleigh, Cali, Calleigh, Cally)
Greek, meaning 'beauty'.

Calliope
Greek, meaning 'beautiful voice'. From the muse of epic poetry in Greek mythology.

Callista
(alt. Callisto)
Greek, meaning 'most beautiful'.

Camas

Native American, from the root and bulb of the same name.

Cambria

Welsh, from the alternative name for Wales.

Camden
(alt. Camdyn)

English, meaning 'winding valley'.

Cameo

Italian, meaning 'skin'.

Cameron
(alt. Camryn)

Scottish Gaelic, meaning 'bent nose'.

Camilla
(alt. Camelia, Camellia, Camila, Camillia)

Latin, meaning 'spiritual serving girl'.

Camille

Latin, meaning 'spiritual serving girl'.

Candace
(alt. Candice, Candis)

Latin, meaning 'brilliant white'.

Candida

Latin, meaning 'white'.

Candra

Latin, meaning 'glowing'.

Candy
(alt. Candi)

Shortened form of Candace, meaning 'brilliant white'.

Canei

Greek, meaning 'pure'.

Caoimhe

Celtic, meaning 'gentleness'.

Caprice

Italian, meaning 'ruled by whim'.

Cara

Latin, meaning 'darling'.

Caren
(alt. Carin, Caron, Caryn)

Greek, meaning 'pure'.

Carey
(alt. Cari, Carie, Carri, Carrie, Cary)
Welsh, meaning 'near the castle'.

Carina
(alt. Corina)
Italian, meaning 'dearest little one'.

Carissa
(alt. Carisa)
Greek, meaning 'grace'.

Carla
(alt. Charla)
Feminine of the Old Norse Carl, meaning 'free man'.

Carlin
(alt. Carleen, Carlene)
Gaelic, meaning 'little champion'.

Carlotta
(alt. Carlota)
Italian form of Charlotte, meaning 'little and feminine'.

Carly
(alt. Carlee, Carley, Carli, Carlie)
Feminine of the German Charles, meaning 'free man'.

Carmel
(alt. Carmela, Carmelita, Carmella)
Hebrew, meaning 'garden'.

Carmen
(alt. Carma, Carmina)
Latin, meaning 'song'.

Carol
(alt. Carole, Carrol, Carroll, Caryl)
Shortened form of Caroline, meaning 'man'.

Caroline
(alt. Carolann, Carolina, Carolyn, Carolynn)
German, meaning 'man'.

Carrington
English, meaning 'Charles's town'.

Carys
(alt. Cerys)
Welsh, meaning 'love'.

Casey
Irish Gaelic, meaning 'watchful'.

Saints' names

Agatha
Agnes
Barbara
Cecilia
Genevieve
Louise
Matilda
Seraphina
Tatiana
Teresa
Vivian

Cassandra
(alt. Casandra, Cassandre)
Greek, meaning 'one who prophesies doom'.

Cassia
(alt. Casia, Casie, Cassie)
Greek, meaning 'cinnamon'.

Cassidy
Irish, meaning 'clever'.

Cassiopeia
(alt. Cassiopia, Cassiopea)
Greek, from the constellation and the Greek myth.

Catalina
(alt. Catarina, Caterina)
Spanish version of Catherine, meaning 'pure'.

Catherine
(alt. Catharine, Cathrine, Cathryn)
Greek, meaning 'pure'.

Cathleen
Irish version of Catherine, meaning 'pure'.

Cathy
(alt. Cathey, Cathi, Cathie)
Shortened form of Catherine, meaning 'pure'.

Caty
(alt. Caddie, Caitee, Cate, Catie)
Shortened form of Catherine, meaning 'pure'.

Cayley
(alt. Cayla, Caylee, Caylen)
American, meaning 'pure'.

Cecile
(alt. Cecilie)
Latin, meaning 'blind one'.

C

Cecilia

(alt. Cecelia, Cecily, Cicely, Cicily)

Latin, meaning 'blind one'.

Celena

Greek, meaning 'goddess of the moon'.

Celeste

(alt. Celestina, Celestine)

Latin, meaning 'heavenly'.

Celine

(alt. Celia, Celina)

French version of Celeste, meaning 'heavenly'.

Cerise

French, meaning 'cherry'.

Chanah

Hebrew, meaning 'grace'.

Chandler

(alt. Chandell)

English, meaning 'candle maker'.

Chandra

(alt. Chanda, Chandry)

Sanskrit, meaning 'like the moon'.

Chanel

(alt. Chanelle)

French, meaning 'pipe'. Most often associated with the designer of the same name.

Chantal

(alt. Chantel, Chantelle, Chantilly)

French, meaning 'stony spot'.

Chardonnay

French, from the wine variety of the same name.

Charis

(alt. Charissa, Charisse)

Greek, meaning 'grace'.

Charity

Latin, meaning 'brotherly love'.

Charlene

(alt. Charleen, Charline)

German, meaning 'man'.

Charlie

(alt. Charlee, Charley, Charlize, Charly)

Shortened form of Charlotte, meaning 'little and feminine'.

Charlotte
(alt. Charnette, Charolette)
French, meaning 'little and feminine'.

Charmaine
Latin, meaning 'clan'.

Charnelle
(alt. Charnell, Charnel, Charnele)
American, meaning 'sparkles'.

Chastity
Latin, meaning 'purity'.

Chava
(alt. Chaya)
Hebrew, meaning 'beloved'.

Chelsea
(alt. Chelsee, Chelsey, Chelsi, Chelsie)
English, meaning 'port or landing place'.

Cher
French, meaning 'beloved'. Most often associated with the singer of the same name.

Cherie
(alt. Cheri, Cherise)
French, meaning 'dear'.

Cherish
(alt. Cherith)
English, meaning 'to treasure'.

Chermona
Hebrew, meaning 'sacred mountain'.

Cherry
(alt. Cherri)
French, meaning 'cherry fruit'.

TV personality names

Alexa (Chung)
Alesha (Dixon)
Cheryl (Cole)
Dannii (Minogue)
Davina (McCall)
Fearne (Cotton)
Holly (Willoughby)
Kirsty (Alsopp)
Myleene (Klass)
Natasha (Kaplinsky)
Tess (Daly)
Trisha (Goddard)

C

Cheryl
(alt. Cheryle)
English, meaning 'little and womanly'.

Chesney
English, meaning 'place to camp'.

Cheyenne
(alt. Cheyanne)
Native American, from the tribe of the same name.

Chiara
(alt. Ceara, Chiarina, Ciara)
Italian, meaning 'light'.

China
From the country of the same name.

Chiquita
Spanish, meaning 'little one'.

Chloe
(alt. Cloe)
Greek, meaning 'pale green shoot'.

Chloris
Greek, meaning 'pale'.

Chris
(alt. Chrissy, Christa, Christie, Christy, Crissy, Cristy)
Shortened form of Christina, meaning 'anointed Christian'.

Christabel
Latin and French, meaning 'fair Christian'. The title of a poem by Coleridge.

Christina
(alt. Christiana, Cristina)
Greek, meaning 'anointed Christian'.

Christine
(alt. Christeen, Christene, Christiane, Christin)
Greek, meaning 'anointed Christian'.

Chuma
Aramaic, meaning 'warmth'.

Ciara
Irish, meaning 'dark beauty'.

Cierra
(alt. Ciera)
Irish, meaning 'black'.

C

Cinderella

French, meaning 'little ash-girl'. Most often associated with the fairytale.

Cindy

(alt. Cinda, Cindi, Cyndi)

Shortened form of Cynthia, meaning 'goddess from the mountain'.

Cinnamon

Greek, from the spice of the same name.

Citlali

(alt. Citlalli)

Aztec, meaning 'star'.

Citrine

Latin, from the gemstone of the same name.

Claire

(alt. Clare)

Latin, meaning 'bright'.

Clara

(alt. Claira)

Latin, meaning 'bright'.

Clarabelle

(alt. Claribel)

Contraction of Clara and Isobel, meaning 'bright' and 'consecrated to God'.

Clarissa

(alt. Clarice, Clarisse)

Variation of Claire, meaning 'bright'.

Clarity

Latin, meaning 'lucid'.

Claudette

Latin, meaning 'lame'.

Claudia

(alt. Claudie, Claudine)

Latin, meaning 'lame'.

Clematis

Greek, meaning 'vine'.

Clementine

(alt. Clemency, Clementina, Clemmie)

Latin, meaning 'mild and merciful'.

Cleopatra

Greek, meaning 'her father's renown'. Most often associated with the Egyptian queen.

Clio
(alt. Cleo, Cliona)

Greek, from the muse of history of the same name.

Clodagh
Irish, meaning 'river'.

Clotilda
(alt. Clothilda, Clothilde, Clotilde)

German, meaning 'renowned battle'.

Clover
English, from the flower of the same name.

Cloud
American, meaning 'lighthearted'.

Coco
Spanish, meaning 'help'.

Cody
English, meaning 'pillow'.

Colleen
(alt. Coleen)

Irish Gaelic, meaning 'girl'.

Collette
(alt. Colette)

Greek and French, meaning 'people of victory'.

Connie
Latin, meaning 'steadfast'.

Constance
(alt. Constanza)

Latin, meaning 'steadfast'.

Consuelo
(alt. Consuela)

Spanish, meaning 'comfort'.

Cora
Greek, meaning 'maiden'.

Coral
(alt. Coralie, Coraline, Corelia, Corene)

Latin, from the marine life of the same name.

Corazon
Spanish, meaning 'heart'.

Cordelia
(alt. Cordia, Cordie)

Latin, meaning 'heart'.

Corey
(alt. Cori, Corrie, Cory)
Irish Gaelic, meaning 'the hollow'.

Corin
(alt. Corine)
Latin, meaning 'spear'.

Corinne
(alt. Corinna, Corrine)
French version of Cora, meaning 'maiden'.

Corliss
English, meaning 'cheery'.

Cornelia
Latin, meaning 'like a horn'.

Cosette
French, meaning 'people of victory'.

Cosima
(alt. Cosmina)
Greek, meaning 'order'.

Courtney
(alt. Cortney)
English, meaning 'court-dweller'.

Creola
French, meaning 'American-born, English descent'.

Crescent
French, meaning 'increasing'.

Cressida
From the heroine in Greek mythology of the same name.

Crystal
(alt. Christal, Chrystal, Cristal)
Greek, meaning 'ice'.

Csilla
Hungarian, meaning 'defences'.

Cynara
Greek, meaning 'thistly plant'.

Cynthia
Greek, meaning 'goddess from the mountain'.

Cyra
Persian, meaning 'sun'.

Cyrilla
Latin, meaning 'lordly'.

 Girls' names

Dacey

Irish Gaelic, meaning 'from the south'.

Dada

Nigerian, meaning 'curly haired'.

Daelan

English, meaning 'aware'.

Dagmar

German, meaning 'day's glory'.

Dagny

Nordic, meaning 'new day'.

Dahlia

Scandinavian, from the flower of the same name.

Dai

Japanese, meaning 'great'.

Daisy

(alt. Dasia)

English, meaning 'eye of the day'.

Dakota

Native American, meaning 'allies'.

Dalia

(alt. Dalila)

Hebrew, meaning 'delicate branch'.

Dallas

Scottish Gaelic, from the village of the same name. Also a city in the USA.

Damaris
Greek, meaning 'calf'.

Damica
(alt. Damika)
French, meaning 'friendly'.

Damita
Spanish, meaning 'little noblewoman'.

Dana
(alt. Dania, Danna, Dayna)
English, meaning 'from Denmark'.

Danae
Greek, from the mythological heroine of the same name.

Danica
(alt. Danika)
Latin, meaning 'from Denmark'.

Danielle
(alt. Danelle, Daniela, Daniella, Danila, Danyelle)
The feminine form of the Hebrew Daniel, meaning 'God is my judge'.

Danita
English, meaning 'God will judge'.

Daphne
(alt. Dafne, Daphna)
Greek, meaning 'laurel tree'.

Dara
Hebrew and Persian, meaning 'wisdom'.

Darby
(alt. Darbi, Darbie)
Irish, meaning 'park with deer'.

Darcie
(alt. Darci, Darcy)
Irish Gaelic, meaning 'dark'.

Daria
Greek, meaning 'rich'.

Darla
English, meaning 'darling'.

Darlene
(alt. Darleen, Darline)
American, meaning 'darling'.

Darva
Slavic, meaning 'honeybee'.

Daryl
(alt. Darryl)

English, originally used as a surname. Often associated with the actress Daryl Hannah.

Davina

Hebrew, meaning 'loved one'. Best known for the TV presenter Davina McCall.

Dawn
(alt. Dawna)

English, meaning 'the dawn'.

Daya

Hebrew, meaning 'bird of prey'.

Deanna
(alt. Dayana, Deana, Deanna, Deanne)

English, meaning 'valley'.

Debbie
(alt. Debbi, Debby, Debi)

Shortened form of Deborah, meaning 'bee'.

Deborah
(alt. Debbra, Debora, Debra, Debrah)

Hebrew, meaning 'bee'.

December

Latin, meaning 'tenth month'.

Decima
(alt. Decia)

Latin, meaning 'tenth'.

Dee

Welsh, meaning 'swarthy'.

Deidre
(alt. Deidra, Deirdre)

Irish, meaning 'raging woman'.

Deja
(alt. Dejah)

French, meaning 'already'.

Delaney

Irish Gaelic, meaning 'offspring of the challenger'.

Delia

Greek, meaning 'from Delos'.

Delilah
(alt. Delina)

Hebrew, meaning 'seductive'.

Della
(alt. Dell)

Shortened form of Adele, meaning 'nobility'.

D

Delores
(alt. Deloris)
Spanish, meaning 'sorrows'.

Delphine
(alt. Delpha, Delphia, Delphina, Delphinia)
Greek, meaning 'dolphin'.

Delta
Greek, meaning 'fourth child'.

Demetria
(alt. Demetrice, Dimitria)
Greek, from the mythological heroine of the same name.

Demi
French, meaning 'half'. Best known for the actress Demi Moore.

Dena
(alt. Deena)
English, meaning 'from the valley'.

Denise
(alt. Denice, Denisa, Denisse)
French, meaning 'follower of Dionysius'.

Derora
Hebrew, meaning 'stream'.

Desdemona
Greek, meaning 'wretchedness'.

Desiree
(alt. Desirae)
French, meaning 'much desired'.

Desma
Greek, meaning 'blinding oath'.

Destiny
(alt. Destany, Destinee, Destiney, Destini)
French, meaning 'fate'.

Deva
Hindi, meaning 'God-like'.

Devin
(alt. Devinne)
Irish Gaelic, meaning 'poet'.

Devon
English, from the county of the same name.

Diamond
English, meaning 'brilliant'.

Diana
(alt. Dian, Diane, Dianna, Dianne)
Roman, meaning 'divine'.

D

Uncommon three-syllable names

Annabel
Cassandra
Dolores
Gloria
Harriet
Imogen
Julia
Marilyn
Miranda
Nigella

Diandra
Greek, meaning 'two males'.

Dilys
Welsh, meaning 'reliable'.

Dimona
Hebrew, meaning 'south'.

Dinah
(alt. Dina)
Hebrew, meaning 'justified'.

Dionne
Greek, from the mythological heroine of the same name.

Divine
Italian, meaning 'heavenly'.

Dixie
French, meaning 'tenth'.

Dodie
Hebrew, meaning 'well-loved'.

Dolly
(alt. Dollie)
Shortened form of Dorothy, meaning 'gift of God'.

Dolores
(alt. Doloris)
Spanish, meaning 'sorrows'.

Dominique
(alt. Domenica, Dominica, Domonique)
Latin, meaning 'Lord'.

Donata
Latin, meaning 'given'.

Donna
(alt. Dona, Donnie)
Italian, meaning 'lady'.

Dora
Greek, meaning 'gift'.

255

Dorcas

Greek, meaning 'gazelle'.

Doreen

(alt. Dorene, Dorine)

Irish Gaelic, meaning 'brooding'.

Doria

Greek, meaning 'of the sea'.

Doris

(alt. Dorris)

Greek, from the region of the same name.

Dorothy

(alt. Dorathy, Doretha, Dorotha, Dorothea, Dorthy)

Greek, meaning 'gift of God'.

Dorrit

(alt. Dorit)

Greek, meaning 'gift of God'.

Dory

(alt. Dori)

French, meaning 'gilded'.

Dottie

(alt. Dotty)

Shortened form of Dorothy, meaning 'gift of God'.

Dove

(alt. Dovie)

English, from the bird of the same name.

Drew

Greek, meaning 'masculine'.

Drusilla

(alt. Drucilla)

Latin, meaning 'of the Drusus clan'.

Dulcie

(alt. Dulce, Dulcia)

Latin, meaning 'sweet'.

Dusty

(alt. Dusti)

Old German, meaning 'brave warrior'. Often associated with the singer Dusty Springfield.

 Girls' names

Eadlin
(alt. Eadlinn, Eadlyn, Eadlen)
Anglo-Saxon, meaning 'royalty'.

Earla
English, meaning 'leader'.

Eartha
English, meaning 'earth'.

Easter
Egyptian, from the festival of the same name.

Ebba
English, meaning 'fortress of riches'.

Ebony
(alt. Eboni)
Latin, meaning 'deep black wood'.

Echo
Greek, meaning 'reflected sound'. From the mythological nymph of the same name.

Eda
(alt. Edda)
English, meaning 'wealthy and happy'.

Edelmira
Spanish, meaning 'admired for nobility'.

Eden
Hebrew, meaning 'pleasure'.

Edie
(alt. Eddie)
Shortened form of Eden, meaning 'pleasure'.

E

Edina

Scottish, meaning 'from Edinburgh'.

Edith

(alt. Edyth)

English, meaning 'prosperity through battle'.

Edna

Hebrew, meaning 'enjoyment'.

Edrea

English, meaning 'wealthy and powerful'.

Edris

(alt. Edriss, Edrys)

Anglo-Saxon, meaning 'prosperous ruler'.

Edwina

English, meaning 'wealthy friend'.

Effie

Greek, meaning 'pleasant speech'.

Eglantine

French, from the shrub of the same name.

Eibhlín

Irish Gaelic, meaning 'shining and brilliant'.

Eileen

Irish, meaning 'shining and brilliant'.

Ekaterina

(alt. Ekaterini)

Slavic, meaning 'pure'.

Elaine

(alt. Elaina, Elayne)

French, meaning 'bright, shining light'.

Elba

Italian, from the island of the same name.

Elberta

English, meaning 'highborn'.

Eldora

Spanish, meaning 'covered with gold'.

Eldoris

(alt. Eldoriss, Eldorys)

Greek, meaning 'woman of the sea'.

Eleanor

(alt. Elana, Elanor, Eleanora)

Greek, meaning 'light'.

E

Electra

(alt. Elektra)

Greek, meaning 'shining'. Also from the myth.

Elfrida

(alt. Elfrieda)

English, meaning 'elf power'.

Eliane

Hebrew, meaning 'Jehovah is God'.

Elise

French, meaning 'my vow to God'.

Elissa

(alt. Elisa)

French, meaning 'pledged to God'.

Eliza

(alt. Elisha)

Hebrew, meaning 'consecrated to God'.

Elizabeth

(alt. Elisabet, Elisabeth, Elizabella, Elizabelle, Elsbeth, Elspeth)

Hebrew, meaning 'consecrated to God'.

Elke

German, meaning 'nobility'.

Ella

German, meaning 'completely'.

Elle

(alt. Ellie)

French, meaning 'she'.

Ellema

(alt. Ellemah, Elema, Ellemma, Elemah)

African, meaning 'dairy farmer'.

Ellen

(alt. Elin, Eline, Ellyn)

Greek, meaning 'shining'.

Ellice

(alt. Elyse)

Greek, meaning 'the Lord is God'.

Elma

(alt. Elna)

Latin, meaning 'soul'.

Elmira

Arabic, meaning 'aristocratic lady'.

Elodie

French, meaning 'marsh flower'.

Eloise

(alt. Elois, Eloisa, Elouise)

French, meaning 'renowned in battle'.

Elsa
(alt. Else, Elsie)
Hebrew, meaning 'consecrated to God'.

Elva
Irish, meaning 'noble'.

Elvina
English, meaning 'noble friend'.

Elvira
(alt. Elvera)
Spanish, from the ancient city of the same name.

Ember
(alt. Embry)
English, meaning 'spark'.

Emeline
German, meaning 'industrious'.

Emerald
English, meaning 'green gemstone'.

Emery
(alt. Emory)
German, meaning 'ruler of work'.

Emiko
(alt. Emuko)
Japanese, meaning 'pretty child'.

Emilia
Latin, meaning 'rival, eager'.

Emily
(alt. Emalee, Emelie, Emely, Emilee, Emilie, Emlyn)
Latin, meaning 'rival, eager'.

Emma
German, meaning 'embraces everything'. The title character of Jane Austen's novel.

Emmanuelle
Hebrew, meaning 'God is among us'.

Emmeline
(alt. Emmelina)
German, meaning 'embraces everything'.

Emmy
(alt. Emi, Emme, Emmie)
German, meaning 'embraces everything'.

Ena
Shortened form of Georgina, meaning 'farmer'.

Enid
(alt. Eneida)
Welsh, meaning 'life spirit'.

Enola
Native American, meaning 'solitary'.

Enya
Irish Gaelic, meaning 'fire'.

Eranthe
Greek, meaning 'delicate like the spring'.

Erica
(alt. Ericka, Erika)
Scandinavian, meaning 'ruler forever'.

Erin
(alt. Eryn)
Irish Gaelic, meaning 'from the isle to the west'.

Eris
Greek, from the mythological heroine of the same name.

Erlinda
Hebrew, meaning 'spirited'.

Erma
German, meaning 'universal'.

Ermine
French, meaning 'weasel'.

Erna
English, meaning 'sincere'.

Ernestine
(alt. Ernestina)
English, meaning 'sincere'.

Esme
French, meaning 'esteemed'.

Esmeralda
Spanish, meaning 'emerald'.

Esperanza
Spanish, meaning 'hope'.

Estelle
(alt. Estela, Estell, Estella)
French, meaning 'star'.

Esther
(alt. Esta, Ester, Etha, Ethna, Ethne)
Persian, meaning 'star'.

Etinia
(alt. Eteniah, Etene, Eteniya)
Native American, meaning 'prosperous'.

Eternity
Latin, meaning 'forever'.

Ethel
(alt. Ethyl)

English, meaning 'noble'.

Etta
(alt. Etter, Ettie)

Shortened form of Henrietta, meaning 'ruler of the house'.

Eudora

Greek, meaning 'generous gift'.

Eugenia
(alt. Eugenie)

Greek, meaning 'well born'.

Eulalia
(alt. Eula, Eulah, Eulalie)

Greek, meaning 'sweet-speaking'.

Eunice

Greek, meaning 'victorious'.

Euphemia

Greek, meaning ' favourable speech'.

Eva

Hebrew, meaning 'life'.

Evadne

Greek, meaning 'pleasing one'.

Evangeline
(alt. Evangelina)

Greek, meaning 'good news'.

Evanthe

Greek, meaning 'good flower'.

Eve
(alt. Evie)

Hebrew, meaning 'life'. The first woman created by God in the Bible.

Evelina
(alt. Evelia)

German, meaning 'hazelnut'.

Evelyn
(alt. Evalyn, Evelin, Eveline, Evelyne)

German, meaning 'hazelnut'.

Everly
(alt. Everleigh, Everley)

English, meaning 'grazing meadow'.

Evette

French, meaning 'yew wood'.

Evonne
(alt. Evon)

French, meaning 'yew wood'.

E

 Girls' names

Fabia
(alt. Fabiana, Fabienne, Fabiola, Fabriana)
Latin, meaning 'from the Fabian clan'.

Fabrizia
Italian, meaning 'works with hands'.

Fahari
Swahili, meaning 'splendour'.

Faith
English, meaning 'loyalty'.

Faiza
Arabic, meaning 'victorious'.

Fallon
Irish Gaelic, meaning 'descended from a ruler'.

Fanny
(alt Fannie)
Latin, meaning 'from France'.

Farica
German, meaning 'peaceful ruler'.

Farrah
English, meaning 'lovely and pleasant'.

Fatima
Arabic, meaning 'baby's nurse'.

Faustine
Latin, meaning 'fortunate'.

Fawn
French, meaning 'young deer'.

Fay
(alt. Fae, Faye)
French, meaning 'fairy'.

Fayola
(alt. Fayolah, Fayeena)
African, meaning 'walks with honour'.

Old name, new fashion?

Arabella
Clara
Clarissa
Dorothy
Evelyn
Hazel
Marjorie
Nora
Penelope
Rosamond

Felicia
(alt. Felecia, Felice, Felicita, Felisha)
Latin, meaning 'lucky and happy'.

Felicity
Latin, meaning 'fortunate'.

Fenella
Irish Gaelic, meaning 'white shoulder'.

Fenia
Scandinavian, from the mythological giantess of the same name.

Fern
(alt. Ferne, Ferrin)
English, from the plant of the same name.

Fernanda
German, meaning 'peace and courage'.

Ffion
(alt. Fion)
Irish Gaelic, meaning 'fair and pale'.

Fia

Italian, meaning 'flame'.

Fifi

Hebrew, meaning 'Jehovah increases'.

Filomena

Greek, meaning 'loved one'.

Finlay

(alt. Finley)

Irish Gaelic, meaning 'fair-headed courageous one'.

Finola

(alt. Fionnula)

Irish Gaelic, meaning 'fair shoulder'.

Fiona

Irish Gaelic, meaning 'fair and pale'.

Fiora

Irish Gaelic, meaning 'fair and pale'.

Fiorella

Italian, meaning 'little flower'.

Flanna

(alt. Flannery)

Irish Gaelic, meaning 'russet hair'.

Flavia

Latin, meaning 'yellow hair'.

Fleur

French, meaning 'flower'.

Flo

(alt. Florrie, Flossie, Floy)

Shortened form of Florence, meaning 'in bloom'.

Flora

Latin, meaning 'flower'.

Florence

(alt. Florencia, Florene, Florine)

Latin, meaning 'in bloom'. Also the Italian city.

Florida

Latin, meaning 'flowery'. Also a state in the USA.

Fran

(alt. Frankie, Frannie)

Shortened form of Frances, meaning 'from France'.

Frances
(alt. Francine, Francis)
Latin, meaning 'from France'.

Francesca
(alt. Franchesca, Francisca)
Latin, meaning 'from France'.

Freda
(alt. Freeda, Freida, Frida, Frieda)
German, meaning 'peaceful'.

Frederica
German, meaning 'peaceful ruler'.

Fuchsia
German, from the flower of the same name.

Fumik
Japanese, meaning 'little friend'.

Names of poets

Amy (Lowell)
Anne (Sexton)
Carol Ann (Duffy)
Charlotte (Smith)
Emily (Dickinson)
Fleur (Adcock)
Gwyneth (Lewis)
Pam (Ayres)
Ruth (Padel)
Sylvia (Plath)
Wendy (Cope)

F

Girls' names

Gabby
(alt. Gabbi)
Shortened form of Gabrielle, meaning 'heroine of God'.

Gabrielle
(alt. Gabriel, Gabriela, Gabriella)
Hebrew, meaning 'heroine of God'.

Gadara
Armenian, meaning 'mountain's peak'.

Gaia
(alt. Gaea)
Greek, meaning 'the earth'.

Gail
(alt. Gale, Gayla, Gayle)
Hebrew, meaning 'my father rejoices'.

Gala
French, meaning 'festive merrymaking'.

Galiena
German, meaning 'high one'.

Galina
Russian, meaning 'shining brightly'.

Garnet
(alt. Garnett)
English, meaning 'red gemstone'.

Gay
(alt. Gaye)
French, meaning 'glad and lighthearted'.

Gaynor

Welsh, meaning 'white and smooth'.

Gemini

Greek, meaning 'twin'. One of the signs of the zodiac.

Gemma

Italian, meaning 'precious stone'.

Gene

Greek, meaning 'wellborn'.

Genesis

Greek, meaning 'beginning'.

Geneva

(alt. Genevra)

French, meaning 'juniper tree'.

Genevieve

German, meaning 'white wave'.

Genie

Shortened form of Genevieve, meaning 'white wave'.

Georgette

French, meaning 'farmer'.

Names from ancient Rome

Agnes
Cecilia
Chloris
Diana
Flavia
Lavinia
Octavia
Paula
Portia
Tatiana

Georgia

(alt. Georgiana, Georgianna, Georgie)

Latin, meaning 'farmer'.

Georgina

(alt. Georgene, Georgine, Giorgina)

Latin, meaning 'farmer'.

Geraldine

German, meaning 'spear ruler'.

Gerda

Nordic, meaning 'shelter'.

Geri
(alt. Gerri, Gerry)
Shortened form of Geraldine, meaning 'spear ruler'.

Germaine
French, meaning 'from Germany'.

Gertie
Shortened form of Gertrude, meaning 'strength of a spear'.

Gertrude
German, meaning 'strength of a spear'.

Ghislaine
French, meaning 'pledge'.

Gia
(alt. Ghia)
Italian, meaning 'God is gracious'.

Gianina
(alt. Giana)
Hebrew, meaning 'God's graciousness'.

Gigi
(alt. Giget)
Shortened form of Georgina, meaning 'farmer'.

Gilda
English, meaning 'gilded'.

Gilia
Hebrew, meaning 'joy of the Lord'.

Gillian
Latin, meaning 'youthful'.

Gina
(alt. Geena, Gena)
Shortened form of Regina, meaning 'queen'.

Ginger
Latin, from the root of the same name.

Ginny
Shortened form of Virginia, meaning 'virgin'.

Giovanna
Italian, meaning 'God is gracious'.

Giselle
(alt. Gisela, Gisele, Giselle, Gisselle)
German, meaning 'pledge'.

Gita

(alt. Geeta)

Sanskrit, meaning 'song'.

Giulia

(alt. Giuliana)

Italian, meaning 'youthful'.

Gladys

(alt. Gladyce)

Welsh, meaning 'lame'.

Glenda

Welsh, meaning 'fair and good'.

Glenna

(alt. Glennie)

Irish Gaelic, meaning 'glen'.

Glenys

Welsh, meaning 'riverbank'.

Gloria

(alt. Glory)

Latin, meaning 'glory'.

Glynda

(alt. Glinda)

Welsh, meaning 'fair'. The good witch in the *Wizard of Oz*.

Glynis

Welsh, meaning 'small glen'.

Golda

(alt. Goldia, Goldie)

English, meaning 'gold'.

Grace

(alt. Graça, Gracie, Gracin, Grayce)

Latin, meaning 'grace'.

Grainne

(alt. Grania)

Irish Gaelic, meaning 'love'.

Gratia

(alt. Grasia)

Latin, meaning 'blessing'.

Greer

(alt. Grier)

Latin, meaning 'alert and watchful'.

Gregoria

Latin, meaning 'alert'.

Greta

(alt. Gretel)

Greek, meaning 'pearl'.

Gretchen

German, meaning 'pearl'.

Griselda

(alt. Griselle)

German, meaning 'grey fighting maid'.

Gudrun

Scandinavian, meaning 'battle'.

Guinevere

Welsh, meaning 'white and smooth'. The queen in Arthurian legend.

Gwen

Shortened form of Gwendolyn, meaning 'fair bow'.

Gwenda

Welsh, meaning 'fair and good'.

Gwendolyn

(alt. Gwendolen, Gwenel)

Welsh, meaning 'fair bow'.

Gwyneth

(alt. Gwynneth, Gwynyth)

Welsh, meaning 'happiness'.

Gwynn

(alt. Gwyn)

Welsh, meaning 'fair blessed'.

Gypsy

English, meaning 'of the Roman tribe'.

Grythao

English, meaning 'fiery'.

Names from ancient Greece

Agatha
Ariadne
Berenice
Cressida
Iliana
Lisandra
Medea
Nereida
Sophia
Xenia

G

English and Scottish royalty

Anna	Mairi
Anne	Margaret
Catherine	Mary
Eleanor	Matilda
Elizabeth	Victoria

Girls' names

Habibah
(alt. Habiba)
Arabic, meaning 'beloved'.

Hadassah
Hebrew, meaning 'myrtle tree'.

Hadley
English, meaning 'heather meadow'.

Hadria
Latin, meaning 'from Adria'.

Hala
Arabic, meaning 'halo'.

Haley
(alt. Haelee, Haely, Hailee, Hailey, Hailie, Haleigh, Hali, Halie)
English, meaning 'hay meadow'.

Halima
(alt. Halina)
Arabic, meaning 'gentle'.

Hallie
(alt. Halle, Halley, Hallie)
German, meaning 'ruler of the home or estate'.

Hannah
(alt. Haana, Hana, Hanna)
Hebrew, meaning 'grace'.

Harika

Turkish, meaning 'superior one'.

Harley
(alt. Harlene)

English, meaning 'the long field'.

Harlow

English, meaning 'army hill'.

Harmony

Latin, meaning 'harmony'.

Harper

English, meaning 'minstrel'.

Harriet
(alt. Harriett, Harriette)

German, meaning 'ruler of the home or estate'.

Hattie

Shortened form of Harriet, meaning 'ruler of the home or estate'.

Haven

English, meaning 'a place of sanctuary'.

Hayden

Old English, meaning 'hedged valley'.

Hayley
(alt. Haylee, Hayleigh, Haylie)

English, meaning 'hay meadow'.

Hazel
(alt. Hazle)

English, from the tree of the same name.

Heather

English, from the flower of the same name.

Heaven

English, meaning 'everlasting bliss'.

Hedda

German, meaning 'warfare'.

Hedwig

German, meaning 'warfare and strife'.

Heidi
(alt. Heidy)

German, meaning 'nobility'.

Helen
(alt. Halen, Helena, Helene, Hellen)
Greek, meaning 'light'.

Helga
German, meaning 'holy and sacred'.

Helia
Greek, meaning 'sun'.

Heloise
French, meaning 'renowned in war'.

Henrietta
(alt. Henriette)
German, meaning 'ruler of the house'.

Hephzibah
Hebrew, meaning 'my delight is in her'.

Hera
Greek, meaning 'queen'. The wife of Zeus in Greek mythology.

Hermia
(alt. Hermina, Hermine, Herminia)
Greek, meaning 'messenger'.

Hermione
Greek, meaning 'earthly'. Best known for the Harry Potter character.

Hero
Greek, meaning 'brave one of the people'.

Hertha
English, meaning 'earth'.

Hesper
(alt. Hesperia)
Greek, meaning 'evening star'.

Hester
(alt. Hestia)
Greek, meaning 'star'.

Hilary
(alt. Hillary)
Greek, meaning 'cheerful and happy'.

Hilda
(alt. Hildur)
German, meaning 'battle woman'.

H

Hildegarde
(alt. Hildegard)

German, meaning 'battle stronghold'.

Hildred

German, meaning 'battle counsellor'.

Hilma

German variant of Wilhelmina, meaning 'helmet'.

Hirkani

Indian, meaning 'like a diamond'.

Hollis

English, meaning 'near the holly bushes'.

Holly
(alt. Holli, Hollie)

English, from the tree of the same name.

Honey

English, from the word 'honey'.

Honor
(alt. Honour)

Latin, meaning 'woman of honour'.

Honora
(alt. Honoria)

Latin, meaning 'woman of honour'.

Hope

English, meaning 'hope'.

Hortense
(alt. Hortencia, Hortensia)

Latin, meaning 'of the garden'.

Hudson

English, meaning 'adventurous'.

Hulda

German, meaning 'loved one'.

Hyacinth

Greek, from the flower of the same name.

Girls' names

Iantha
Greek, meaning 'purple flower'.

Ichigo
Japanese, meaning 'strawberry'.

Ida
English, meaning 'prosperous'.

Idell
(alt. Idella)
English, meaning 'prosperous'.

Idona
Nordic, meaning 'renewal'.

Ignacia
Latin, meaning 'ardent'.

Ila
French, meaning 'island'.

Ilana
Hebrew, meaning 'tree'.

Ilaria
Italian, meaning 'cheerful'.

Ilene
American, meaning 'light'.

Iliana
(alt. Ileana)
Greek, meaning 'Trojan'.

Ilona
Hungarian, meaning 'light'.

Ilsa

German, meaning 'pledged to God'.

Ima

German, meaning 'embraces everything'.

Iman

Arabic, meaning 'faith'.

Imara

Hungarian, meaning 'great ruler'.

Imelda

German, meaning 'all-consuming fight'.

Imogen

(alt. Imogene)

Latin, meaning 'last-born'.

Ina

Latin, meaning 'to make feminine'.

Inaya

Arabic, meaning 'taking care'.

India

(alt. Indie)

Hindi, from the country of the same name.

Indiana

Latin, meaning 'from India'. Also a state in the USA.

Indigo

Greek, meaning 'deep blue dye'.

Indira

(alt. Inira)

Sanskrit, meaning 'beauty'.

Inez

(alt. Ines)

Spanish, meaning 'pure'.

Inga

(alt. Inge, Ingeborg, Inger)

Scandinavian, meaning 'guarded by Ing'.

Ingrid

Scandinavian, meaning 'beautiful'.

Io

(alt. Eyo)

Greek, from the mythological heroine of the same name.

Ioanna

Greek, meaning 'grace'.

Iola

(alt. Iole)

Greek, meaning 'cloud of dawn'.

Iolanthe

Greek, meaning 'violet flower'.

Iona

Greek, from the island of the same name.

Ione

Greek, meaning 'violet'.

Iorwen

Welsh, meaning 'fair'.

Iphigenia

Greek, meaning 'sacrifice'.

Ira

(alt. Iva)

Hebrew, meaning 'watchful'.

Irene

(alt. Irelyn, Irena, Irina, Irini)

Greek, meaning 'peace'.

Iris

Greek, meaning 'rainbow'. Also from the flower of the same name.

Irma

German, meaning 'universal'.

Isabel

(alt. Isabela, Isabell, Isabella, Isabelle, Isabeth, Isobel, Izabella, Izabelle)

Spanish, meaning 'pledged to God'.

Isadora

Latin, meaning 'gift of Isis'.

Ishana

Hindi, meaning 'desire'.

Isis

Egyptian, from the goddess of the same name.

Isla

(alt. Isa, Isela, Isley)

Scottish Gaelic, meaning 'river'.

Isolde

Welsh, meaning 'fair lady'.

Istas

Native American, meaning 'snow'.

Ivana

Slavic, meaning 'Jehovah is gracious'.

Ivette

Variation of Yvette, meaning 'yew wood'.

Ivonne

Variation of Yvonne, meaning 'yew wood'.

Ivory

Latin, meaning 'white as elephant tusks'.

Ivy

English, from the plant of the same name.

Ixia

South African, from the flower of the same name.

Boys' names for girls (female spellings)

Alex
Billie
Cori
Charlie
Elliott
Geri
Jamie
Jo
Leslie
Robyn
Toni

 Girls' names

Jaamini
Hindi, meaning 'evening'.

Jacinda
(alt. Jacinta)
Spanish, meaning 'hyacinth'.

Jackie
(alt. Jacque, Jacqui)
Shortened form of Jacqueline, meaning 'he who supplants'.

Jacqueline
(alt. Jacalyn, Jacklyn, Jaclyn, Jacquelin, Jacquelyn, Jacquline, Jaqlyn, Jaquelin, Jaqueline)
French, meaning 'he who supplants'.

Jade
(alt. Jada, Jaida, Jayda, Jayde)
Spanish, meaning 'green stone'.

Jaden
(alt. Jadyn, Jaiden, Jaidyn, Jayden)
Contraction of Jade and Hayden, meaning 'green hedged valley'.

Jael
Hebrew, meaning 'mountain goat'.

Jaime
(alt. Jaima, Jaimie, Jami, Jamie)
Spanish, meaning 'he who supplants'.

Jamila
Arabic, meaning 'lovely'.

Jan
(alt. Jann, Janna)

Hebrew, meaning 'the Lord is gracious'.

Jana
(alt. Jaana)

Hebrew, meaning 'the Lord is gracious'.

Janae
(alt. Janay)

American, meaning 'the Lord is gracious'.

Jane
(alt. Jayne)

Feminine form of the Hebrew John, meaning 'the Lord is gracious'.

Janelle
(alt. Janel, Janell, Jenelle)

American, meaning 'the Lord is gracious'.

Janet
(alt. Janette)

Scottish, meaning 'the Lord is gracious'.

Janice
(alt. Janis)

American, meaning 'the Lord is gracious'.

Janie
(alt. Janney, Jannie)

Shortened form of Janet, meaning 'the Lord is gracious'.

Janine
(alt. Janeen)

English, meaning 'the Lord is gracious'.

Janoah
(alt. Janiya, Janiyah)

Hebrew, meaning 'quiet and calm'.

January
Latin, meaning 'the first month'.

Jarita
Hindi-Sanskrit, meaning 'famous bird'.

Jasmine
(alt. Jasmin, Jazim, Jazmine)

Persian, meaning 'jasmine flower'.

J

Jay

Latin, meaning 'jaybird'.

Jayna

Sanskrit, meaning 'bringer of victory'.

Jean

(alt. Jeane, Jeanne)

Scottish, meaning 'the Lord is gracious'.

Jeana

(alt. Jeanna)

Latin, meaning 'queen'.

Jeanette

(alt. Jeannette, Janette)

French, meaning 'the Lord is gracious'.

Jeanie

(alt. Jeannie)

Shortened form of Jeanette, meaning 'the Lord is gracious'.

Jeanine

(alt. Jeannine)

Latin, meaning 'the Lord is gracious'.

Jemima

Hebrew, meaning 'dove'.

Jemma

Italian, meaning 'precious stone'.

Jena

Arabic, meaning 'little bird'.

Jenna

Hebrew, meaning 'the Lord is gracious'.

Jennifer

(alt. Jenifer)

Welsh, meaning 'white and smooth'.

Flower names

Acacia
Bluebell
Daisy
Flora
Hyacinth
Lilac
Petunia
Primrose
Rose
Snowdrop

J

Jenny
(alt. Jennie)
Shortened form of Jennifer, meaning 'white and smooth'.

Jerrie
(alt. Jeri, Jerri, Jerrie, Jerry)
German, meaning 'spear ruler'.

Jerusha
Hebrew, meaning 'married'.

Jeryl
English, meaning 'spear ruler'.

Jessa
Shortened form of Jessica, meaning 'He sees'.

Jessamy
(alt. Jessame, Jessamine, Jessamyn)
Persian, meaning 'jasmine flower'.

Jessica
(alt. Jesica, Jesika, Jessika)
Hebrew, meaning 'He sees'.

Jessie
(alt. Jesse, Jessi, Jessye)
Shortened form of Jessica, meaning 'He sees'.

Jesusa
Spanish, meaning 'mother of the Lord'.

Jethetha
Hebrew, meaning 'princess'.

Jette
(alt. Jetta, Jettie)
Danish, meaning 'black as coal'.

Jewel
(alt. Jewell)
French, meaning 'delight'.

Jezebel
(alt. Jezabel, Jezabelle)
Hebrew, meaning 'pure and virginal'. Now often used as a term for bad women.

Jill
Latin, meaning 'youthful'.

Jillian
Latin, meaning 'youthful'.

Jimena
Spanish, meaning 'heard'.

Jo

Shortened form of Joanna, meaning 'the Lord is gracious'.

Joan

Hebrew, meaning 'the Lord is gracious'.

Joanna

(alt. Joana, Joanie, Joann, Joanne, Johanna, Joni)

Hebrew, meaning 'the Lord is gracious'.

Jocasta

Italian, meaning 'lighthearted'.

Jocelyn

(alt. Jauslyn, Jocelyne, Joscelin, Joslyn)

German, meaning 'cheerful'.

Jody

(alt. Jodee, Jodi, Jodie)

Shortened form of Judith, meaning 'Jewish'.

Joelle

(alt. Joela)

Hebrew, meaning 'Jehovah is the Lord'.

Joie

French, meaning 'joy'.

Jolene

Contraction of Joanna and Darlene, meaning 'gracious darling'.

Jolie

(alt. Joely)

French, meaning 'pretty'.

Jordan

(alt. Jordana, Jordin, Jordyn)

Hebrew, meaning 'descend'.

Josephine

(alt. Josefina, Josephina)

Hebrew, meaning 'Jehovah increases'.

Josie

(alt. Joss, Jossie)

Shortened form of Josephine, meaning 'Jehovah increases'.

Jovita

(alt. Jovie)

Latin, meaning 'made glad'.

Joy

Latin, meaning 'joy'.

Joyce

Latin, meaning 'joyous'.

Juanita
(alt. Juana)

Spanish, meaning 'the Lord is gracious'.

Jubilee

Hebrew, meaning 'horn of a ram'.

Judith
(alt. Judit)

Hebrew, meaning 'Jewish'.

Judy
(alt. Judi, Judie)

Shortened form of Judith, Hebrew, meaning 'Jewish'.

Jules

French, meaning 'Jove's child'.

Julia

Latin, meaning 'youthful'.

Julianne
(alt. Juliana, Juliann, Julianne)

Latin, meaning 'youthful'

Julie
(alt. Juli)

Shortened form of Julia, meaning 'youthful'.

Juliet
(alt. Joliet, Juliette)

Latin, meaning 'youthful'. Most often associated with Shakespeare's heroine.

June
(alt. Juna)

Latin, after the month of the same name.

Juniper

Dutch, from the shrub of the same name.

Juno
(alt. Juneau)

Latin, meaning 'queen of heaven'.

Justice

English, meaning 'to deliver what is just'.

Justine
(alt. Justina)

Latin, meaning 'fair and righteous'.

Jørgina

Dutch, meaning 'farmer'.

K Girls' names

Kadenza
(alt. Kadence)
Latin, meaning 'with rhythm'.

Kadisha
Hebrew, meaning 'religious one'.

Kaitlin
(alt. Kaitlyn)
Greek, meaning 'pure'.

Kala
(alt. Kaela, Kaiala, Kaila)
Sanskrit, meaning 'black one'.

Kali
(alt. Kailee, Kailey, Kaleigh, Kaley, Kalie, Kalli, Kally, Kaylee, Kayleigh)
Sanskrit, meaning 'black one'.

Kalila
Arabic, meaning 'beloved'.

Kalina
Slavic, meaning 'flower'.

Kalliope
(alt. Calliope)
Greek, meaning 'beautiful voice'. From the muse of the same name.

Kallista
Greek, meaning 'most beautiful'.

Kama
Sanskrit, meaning 'love'.

Kami
Japanese, meaning 'lord'.

Place names

Adelaide
Atlanta
Brittany
Etna
Florence
India
Lydia
Madeira
Paris
Savannah

Kamilla
(alt. Kamilah)

Slavic, meaning 'serving girl'.

Kana

Hawaiian, from the demi-god of the same name.

Kandace
(alt. Kandice)

Latin, meaning 'glowing white'.

Kandy
(alt. Kandi)

Shortened form of Kandace, meaning 'glowing white'.

Kanika

African, meaning 'black cloth'.

Kara

Latin, meaning 'dear one'.

Karen
(alt. Karan, Karalyn, Karin, Karina, Karon, Karren)

Greek, meaning 'pure'.

Kari
(alt. Karie, Karri, Karrie)

Shortened form of Karen, meaning 'pure'.

Karimah

Arabic, meaning 'giving'.

Karishma

Sanskrit, meaning 'miracle'.

Karla

German, meaning 'man'.

Karly
(alt. Karlee, Karley, Karli)

German, meaning 'free man'.

Karlyn

German, meaning 'man'.

Karma

Hindi, meaning 'destiny'.

Karol
(alt. Karolina, Karolyn)
Slavic, meaning 'little and womanly'.

Kasey
(alt. Kacey, Kaci, Kacie, Kacy, Kasie, Kassie)
Irish Gaelic, meaning 'alert and watchful'.

Kassandra
Greek, meaning 'she who entangles men'.

Kasumi
Japanese, meaning 'of the mist'.

Katarina
(alt. Katarine, Katerina, Katharina)
Greek, meaning 'pure'.

Kate
(alt. Kat, Katie, Kathi, Kathie, Kathy, Kati, Katy)
Shortened form of Katherine, meaning 'pure'.

Katelyn
(alt. Katelin, Katelynn, Katlin, Katlyn)
Greek, meaning 'pure'.

Katherine
(alt. Katharine, Katheryn, Kathrine, Kathryn)
Greek, meaning 'pure'.

Kathleen
(alt. Kathlyn)
Greek, meaning 'pure'.

Katrina
(alt. Katina)
Greek, meaning 'pure'.

Kaveri
Indian, meaning 'sacred river'.

Kay
(alt. Kaye)
Shortened form of Katherine, meaning 'pure'.

Kaya
Sanskrit, meaning 'nature', or Turkish, meaning 'rock'.

Kayla
(alt. Kaylah)
Greek, meaning 'pure'.

Kayley
(alt. Kayley, Kayli)
American, meaning 'pure'.

Kaylin
American, meaning 'pure'.

289

Keeley
(alt. Keely)
Irish, meaning 'battle maid'.

Keila
Hebrew, meaning 'citadel'.

Keira
Irish Gaelic, meaning 'dark'.

Keisha
(alt. Keesha)
Arabic, meaning 'woman'.

Kelis
American, meaning 'beautiful'.

Kelly
(alt. Keli, Kelley, Kelli, Kellie)
Irish Gaelic, meaning 'battle maid'.

Kelsey
(alt. Kelcee, Kelcie, Kelsea, Kelsi, Kelsie)
English, meaning 'island'.

Kendall
(alt. Kendal)
English, meaning 'the valley of the River Kent'. Also a place in Cumbria.

Kendra
English, meaning 'knowing'.

Kenna
Irish Gaelic, meaning 'handsome'.

Kennedy
(alt. Kenadee, Kennedi)
Irish Gaelic, meaning 'helmet head'.

Kenya
African, from the country of the same name.

Kerensa
Cornish, meaning 'love'.

Kerrigan
Irish, meaning 'black haired'.

Kerry
(alt. Keri, Kerri, Kerrie)
Irish, from the county of the same name.

Khadijah
(alt. Khadejah)
Arabic, meaning 'premature baby'.

Kiana
(alt. Kia, Kiana)
American, meaning 'fibre'.

Kiara

Italian, meaning 'light'.

Kiki

Spanish, meaning 'home ruler'.

Kim

Shortened form of Kimberly, from the town of the same name.

Kimana

Native American, meaning 'butterfly'.

Kimberly

(alt. Kimberleigh, Kimberley)

Old English, meaning 'royal forest'.

Kingsley

(alt. Kinsley)

English, meaning 'king's meadow'.

Kinsey

English, meaning 'king's victory'.

Kira

Greek, meaning 'lady'.

Kiri

Maori, meaning 'tree bark'.

Long names

Alexandra
Benedicta
Christabelle
Constantine
Emmanuelle
Gabrielle
Henrietta
Philomena
Rosamond
Virginia

Kirsten

(alt. Kirstin)

Scandinavian, meaning 'Christian'.

Kirstie

(alt. Kirsty)

Shortened form of Kirsten, meaning 'Christian'.

Kitty

(alt. Kittie)

Shortened form of Katherine, meaning 'pure'.

Kizzy

Hebrew, meaning the plant 'cassia'.

K

Klara
Hungarian, meaning 'bright'.

Komal
Hindi, meaning 'soft and tender'.

Konstantina
Latin, meaning 'steadfast'.

Kora
(alt. Kori)
Greek, meaning 'maiden'.

Kris
(alt. Krista, Kristi, Kristie, Kristy)
Shortened form of Kristen, meaning 'Christian'.

Kristen
(alt. Kristan, Kristin, Kristine, Krysten)
Greek, meaning 'Christian'.

Krystal
(alt. Kristal, Kristel)
Greek, meaning 'ice'.

Kwanza
(alt. Kwanzaa)
African, meaning 'beginning'.

Kyla
(alt. Kya, Kylah, Kyle)
Scottish, meaning 'narrow spit of land'.

Kylie
(alt. Kiley, Kylee)
Irish Gaelic, meaning 'graceful'.

Kyoko
Japanese, meaning 'girl who sees her own true image'.

Kyra
Greek, meaning 'lady'.

Kyrie
Greek, meaning 'the Lord'.

Short names

Ali
Bev
Fay
Jan
Jo
Kay
Lyn
May
Nia
Val

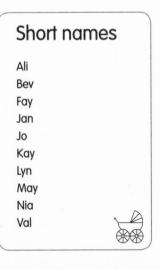

K

L Girls' names

Lacey
(alt. *Laci, Lacie, Lacy*)

French, from a nobleman's surname.

Ladonna
Italian, meaning 'lady'.

Lady
English, meaning 'bread kneader'.

Laidh
Hebrew, meaning 'lioness'.

Laila
(alt. *Laelia, Layla, Leila, Lela, Lelah, Lelia*)

Arabic, meaning 'night'.

Lainey
(alt. *Laine, Laney*)

French, meaning 'bright light'.

Lakeisha
(alt. *Lakeshia*)

American, meaning 'woman'.

Lakshmi
(alt. *Laxmi*)

Sanskrit, meaning 'good omen'. Also the Hindu goddess.

Lana
Greek, meaning 'light'.

Lani
(alt. *Lanie*)

Hawaiian, meaning 'sky'.

Lara
Latin, meaning 'famous'.

Laraine

French, meaning 'from Lorraine'.

Larissa

(alt. Larisa)

Greek, meaning 'lighthearted'.

Lark

(alt. Larkin)

English, meaning 'playful songbird'.

Larsen

Scandinavian, meaning 'son of Lars'.

Latifa

Arabic, meaning 'gentle and pleasant'.

Latika

(alt. Lotika)

Hindi, meaning 'a plant'.

Latisha

Latin, meaning 'happiness'.

Latona

(alt. Latonia)

Roman, from the mythological heroine of the same name.

Latoya

Spanish, meaning 'victorious one'.

Latrice

(alt. Latricia)

Latin, meaning 'noble'.

Laura

Latin, meaning 'laurel'.

Laurel

Latin, meaning 'laurel tree'.

Lauren

(alt. Lauran, Loren)

Latin, meaning 'laurel'.

Laveda

(alt. Lavada)

Latin, meaning 'cleansed'.

Lavender

Latin, from the plant of the same name.

Laverne

(alt. Lavern, Laverna)

Latin, from the goddess of the same name.

Lavinia
(alt. Lavina)

Latin, meaning 'woman of Rome'.

Lavita

American, meaning 'charming'.

Lavonne
(alt. Lavon)

French, meaning 'yew wood'.

Leah
(alt. Lea, Leia)

Hebrew, meaning 'weary'.

Leandra

Greek, meaning 'lion man'.

Leanne
(alt. Leann, Leanna, Leeann)

Contraction of Lee and Ann, meaning 'meadow grace'.

Leda

Greek, meaning 'gladness'.

Lee
(alt. Leigh)

English, meaning 'pasture or meadow'.

'Bad girl' names

Desdemona
Diva
Fifi
Lilith
Pandora
Peaches
Sadie
Scarlett
Tallulah
Xena

Leilani

Hawaiian, meaning 'flower from heaven'.

Leith

Scottish Gaelic, meaning 'broad river'.

Lena
(alt. Leena, Lina)

Latin, meaning 'light'.

Lenna
(alt. Lennie)

German, meaning 'lion's strength'.

Lenore
(alt. Lenora)

Greek, meaning 'light'.

L

Léonie
(alt. Leona, Leone)
Latin, meaning 'lion'.

Leonora
(alt. Leonor, Leonore)
Greek, meaning 'light'.

Leora
Greek, meaning 'light'.

Lerola
Latin, meaning 'like a blackbird'.

Leslie
(alt. Leslee, Lesley, Lesli)
Scottish Gaelic, meaning 'the grey castle'.

Leta
Latin, meaning 'glad and joyful'.

Letha
Greek, meaning 'forgetfulness'.

Letitia
(alt. Leticia, Lettice, Lettie)
Latin, meaning 'joy and gladness'.

Lexia
(alt. Lexie)
Greek, meaning 'defender of mankind'.

Lia
Italian, meaning 'bringer of the gospel'.

Liana
French, meaning 'to twine around'.

Libby
(alt. Libbie)
Shortened form of Elizabeth, meaning 'consecrated to God'.

Liberty
English, meaning 'freedom'.

Lida
Slavic, meaning 'loved by the people'.

Liese
(alt. Liesel, Liesl)
German, meaning 'pledged to God'.

Lila
(alt. Lilah)
Arabic, meaning 'night'.

Lilac

Latin, from the flower of the same name.

Lilia

(alt. Lilias)

Scottish, meaning 'lily'.

Lilith

Arabic, meaning 'ghost'.

Lillian

(alt. Lilian, Liliana, Lilla, Lillianna)

Latin, meaning 'lily'.

Lily

(alt. Lillie, Lilly)

Latin, from the flower of the same name.

Linda

(alt. Lynda)

Spanish, meaning 'pretty'.

Linden

(alt. Lindie, Lindy)

European, from the tree of the same name.

Lindsay

(alt. Lindsey, Linsey)

English, meaning 'island of linden trees'.

Linette

Welsh, meaning 'idol'.

Linnea

(alt. Linnae, Linny)

Scandinavian, meaning 'lime or linden tree'.

Liora

(alt. Lior)

Hebrew, meaning 'I have a light'.

Lirit

Hebrew, meaning 'musically talented'.

Lisa

(alt. Leesa, Lise, Liza)

Hebrew, meaning 'pledged to God'.

Lissa

Greek, meaning 'bee'.

Lissandra

(alt. Lisandra)

Greek, meaning 'man's defender'.

Liv

Nordic, meaning 'defence'.

Famous female singers

Adele (Adkins)
Annie (Lennox)
Billie (Holiday)
Dinah (Washington)
Ella (Fitzgerald)
Etta (James)
Florence (Welch)
Judy (Garland)
Kate (Bush)
Kylie (Minogue)
Lily (Allen)
Nina (Simone)

Livia
Latin, meaning 'olive'.

Liz
(alt. Lizzie, Lizzy)
Shortened form of Elizabeth, meaning 'consecrated to God'.

Logan
Irish Gaelic, meaning 'small hollow'.

Lois
German, meaning 'renowned in battle'.

Lola
Spanish, meaning 'sorrows'.

Lolita
Spanish, meaning 'sorrows'.

Lona
Latin, meaning 'lion'.

Lora
Latin, meaning 'laurel'.

Lorelei
(alt. Loralai, Loralie)
German, meaning 'dangerous rock'.

Lorenza
Latin, meaning 'from Laurentium'.

Loretta
(alt. Loreto)
Latin, meaning 'laurel'.

Lori
(alt. Laurie, Lorie, Lorri)
Latin, meaning 'laurel'.

Lorna
Scottish, from the town of Lorne.

Lorraine
(alt. Loraine)
French, meaning 'from Lorraine'.

Lottie
(alt. Lotta, Lotte)
French, meaning 'little and womanly'.

Lotus
Greek, meaning 'lotus flower'.

Lou
(alt. Louie, Lue)
Shortened form of Louise, meaning 'renowned in battle'.

Louise
(alt. Louisa, Luisa)
German, meaning 'renowned in battle'.

Lourdes
French, from the town of the same name.

Love
English, from the word 'love'.

Lowri
Welsh, meaning 'crowned with laurels'.

Luanne
(alt. Luann, Luanna)
German, meaning 'renowned in battle'.

Luba
Hebrew, meaning 'dearly loved'.

Lucia
(alt. Luciana)
Italian, meaning 'light'.

Lucille
(alt. Lucile, Lucilla)
French, meaning 'light'.

Lucinda
English, meaning 'light'.

Lucretia
(alt. Lucrece)
Spanish, meaning 'light'.

Lucy
(alt. Lucie)
Latin, meaning 'light'.

Ludmilla
Slavic, meaning 'beloved of the people'.

Luella
(alt. Lue)

English, meaning 'renowned in battle'.

Lulu
(alt. Lula)

German, meaning 'renowned in battle'.

Luna

Latin, meaning 'moon'.

Lupita

Spanish, short form of Guadelupe. From the town of the same name.

Luz

Spanish, meaning 'light'.

Lydia
(alt. Lidia)

Greek, meaning 'from Lydia'.

Lynn
(alt. Lyn, Lynne)

Spanish, meaning 'pretty'; English, meaning 'waterfall'.

Lynton

English, meaning 'town of lime trees'.

Lyra

Latin, meaning 'lyre'.

Tennis players

Anna (Kournikova)
Billie Jean (King)
Justine (Henin)
Maria (Sharapova)
Monica (Seles)
Serena (Williams)
Sue (Barker)
Steffi (Graf)
Venus (Williams)

 Girls' names

Mab

Irish Gaelic, meaning 'joy'.

Mabel

(alt. Mabelle, Mable)
Latin, meaning 'loveable'.

Macaria

Spanish, meaning 'blessed'.

Machiko

Japanese, meaning 'beautiful woman'.

Macy

(alt. Macey, Maci, Macie)
French, meaning 'Matthew's estate'.

Mada

English, meaning 'from Magdala'.

Madaio

Hawaiian, meaning 'gift from God'.

Madden

(alt. Maddyn)
Irish, meaning 'little dog'.

Maddie

(alt. Maddi, Maddie, Madie)
Shortened form of Madeline, meaning 'from Magdala'.

Madeline

(alt. Madaline, Madalyn, Madeleine, Madelyn, Madelynn, Madilyn)
Greek, meaning 'from Magdala'.

Madge

Greek, meaning 'pearl'.

Madhuri
Hindi, meaning 'sweet girl'.

Madison
(alt. Maddison, Madisen, Madisyn, Madyson)
English, meaning 'son of the mighty warrior'.

Madonna
Latin, meaning 'my lady'.

Maeve
Irish Gaelic, meaning 'intoxicating'.

Mafalda
Spanish, meaning 'battle-mighty'.

Magali
Greek, meaning 'pearl'.

Magdalene
(alt. Magdalen, Magdalena)
Greek, meaning 'from Magdala'.

Maggie
Shortened form of Margaret, meaning 'pearl'.

Magnolia
Latin, from the flower of the same name.

Mahala
(alt. Mahalia)
Hebrew, meaning 'tender affection'.

Maia
(alt. Maja)
Greek, meaning 'mother'.

Maida
English, meaning 'maiden'.

Maisie
(alt. Maisey, Maisy, Maizie, Masie, Mazie)
Greek, meaning 'pearl'.

Malka
Hebrew, meaning 'queen'.

Mallory
(alt. Malorie)
French, meaning 'unhappy'.

Malvina
Gaelic, meaning 'smooth brow'.

Mamie
(alt. Mammie)
Shortened form of Margaret, meaning 'pearl'.

Mandy
(alt. Mandie)
Shortened form of Amanda, meaning 'much loved'.

Manisha
Sanskrit, meaning 'desire'.

Mansi
Hopi, meaning 'plucked flower'.

Manuela
Spanish, meaning 'the Lord is among us'.

Mara
Hebrew, meaning 'bitter'.

Marcela
(alt. Marceline, Marcella, Marcelle)
Latin, meaning 'war-like'.

Marcia
Latin, meaning 'war-like'.

Marcy
(alt. Marci, Marcie)
Latin, meaning 'war-like'.

Margaret
(alt. Margarete, Margaretta, Margarette, Margret)
Greek, meaning 'pearl'.

Margery
(alt. Marge, Margie, Margit, Margy)
French, meaning 'pearl'.

Margo
(alt. Margot)
French, meaning 'pearl'.

Marguerite
(alt. Margarita)
French, meaning 'pearl'.

Maria
(alt. Mariah)
Latin, meaning 'bitter'.

Marian
(alt. Mariam, Mariana, Marion)
French, meaning 'bitter grace'.

M

Marianne
(alt. Mariana, Mariann, Maryann, Maryanne)
French, meaning 'bitter grace'.

Maribel
American, meaning 'bitterly beautiful'.

Marie
French, meaning 'bitter'.

Mariel
(alt. Mariela, Mariella)
Dutch, meaning 'bitter'.

Marietta
(alt. Marieta)
French, meaning 'bitter'.

Marigold
English, from the flower of the same name.

Marika
Dutch, meaning 'bitter'.

Marilyn
(alt. Marilee, Marilene, Marilynn)
English, meaning 'bitter'.

Marin
American, from the county of the same name.

Marina
(alt. Marine)
Latin, meaning 'from the sea'.

Mariposa
Spanish, meaning 'butterfly'.

Maris
Latin, meaning 'of the sea'.

Marisa
Latin, meaning 'of the sea'.

Marisol
Spanish, meaning 'bitter sun'.

Marissa
American, meaning 'of the sea'.

Marjolaine
French, meaning 'marjoram'.

Marjorie
(alt. Marjory)
French, meaning 'pearl'.

Marla
Shortened form of Marlene, meaning 'bitter'.

Marlene
(alt. Marlen, Marlena)
Hebrew, meaning 'bitter'.

Marley
(alt. Marlee)
American, meaning 'bitter'.

Marlo
(alt. Marlowe)
American, meaning 'bitter'.

Marseille
French, from the city of the same name.

Marsha
English, meaning 'war-like'.

Martha
(alt. Marta)
Aramaic, meaning 'lady'.

Martina
Latin, meaning 'war-like'.

Marvel
French, meaning 'something to marvel at'.

Mary
Hebrew, meaning 'bitter'.

Masada
Hebrew, meaning 'foundation'.

Matilda
(alt. Mathilda, Mathilde, Matide)
German, meaning 'battle-mighty'.

Mattea
Hebrew, meaning 'gift of God'.

Maude
(alt. Maud)
German, meaning 'battle-mighty'.

Maura
Irish, meaning 'bitter'.

Maureen
(alt. Maurine)
Irish, meaning 'bitter'.

Mavis
French, meaning 'thrush'.

Maxine
(alt. Maxie)
Latin, meaning 'greatest'.

M

May

(alt. Mae, Maya, Maye, Mayra)
Hebrew, meaning 'gift of God'.
Also the month.

Mckenna

(alt. Mackenna)
Irish Gaelic, meaning 'son of
the handsome one'.

Mckenzie

(alt. Mackenzie, Mckenzy,
Mikenzi)
Irish Gaelic, meaning 'son of
the wise ruler'.

Meara

Gaelic, meaning 'filled with
happiness'.

Medea

(alt. Meda)
Greek, meaning 'ruling'.

Meg

Shortened form of Margaret,
meaning 'pearl'.

Megan

(alt. Meagan, Meghan)
Welsh, meaning 'pearl'.

Mehitabel

Hebrew, meaning 'benefited
by God'.

Mehri

Persian, meaning 'kind'.

Meiwei

Chinese, meaning 'forever
enchanting'.

Melanie

(alt. Melania, Melany, Melonie)
Greek, meaning 'dark-skinned'.

Melba

Australian, meaning 'from
Melbourne'.

Melia

(alt. Meliah)
German, meaning 'industrious'.

Melina

Greek, meaning 'honey'.

Melinda

Latin, meaning 'honey'.

Melisande

French, meaning 'bee'.

M

Melissa
(alt. *Melisa, Mellissa*)
Greek, meaning 'bee'.

Melody
(alt. *Melodie*)
Greek, meaning 'song'.

Melvina
Celtic, meaning 'chieftain'.

Menora
Hebrew, meaning 'candlestick'.

Mercedes
Spanish, meaning 'mercies'.
Most often associated with the car.

Mercy
English, meaning 'mercy'.

Meredith
(alt. *Meridith*)
Welsh, meaning 'great ruler'.

Merle
French, meaning 'blackbird'.

Merry
English, meaning 'lighthearted'.

Meryl
(alt. *Merrill*)
Irish Gaelic, meaning 'sea-bright'.

Meta
German, meaning 'pearl'.

Mia
Italian, meaning 'mine'.

Michaela
(alt. *Makaela, Makaila, Micaela, Mikaila, Mikayla*)
Hebrew, meaning 'who is like the Lord'.

Michelle
(alt. *Machelle, Mechelle, Michaele, Michal, Michele*)
French, meaning 'who is like the Lord'.

Mickey
(alt. *Mickie*)
Shortened form of Michelle, meaning 'who is like the Lord'.

Mieko
Japanese, meaning 'born into wealth'.

Migdalia
Greek, meaning 'from Magdala'.

Mignon
French, meaning 'cute'.

307

Mika
(alt. Micah)
Hebrew, meaning 'who resembles God'.

Milada
Czech, meaning 'my love'.

Milagros
Spanish, meaning 'miracles'.

Milan
Italian, from the city of the same name.

Mildred
English, meaning 'gentle strength'.

Milena
Czech, meaning 'love and warmth'.

Miley
American, meaning 'smiley'. Made popular by Miley Cyrus.

Millicent
German, meaning 'high-born power'.

Millie
(alt. Milly)
Shortened form of Millicent, meaning 'high-born power'.

Mimi
Italian, meaning 'bitter'.

Popular song names

Alice ('All the Girls Love Alice', Elton John)
Billie Jean ('Billie Jean', Michael Jackson)
Caroline ('Sweet Caroline', Neil Diamond)
Delilah ('Delilah', Tom Jones)
Eileen ('Come on Eileen', Dexy's Midnight Runners)
Eleanor ('Eleanor Rigby', The Beatles)
Judy ('Judy', The Beach Boys)
Roxanne ('Roxanne', The Police)
Sally ('Mustang Sally', Wilson Pickett)
Valerie ('Valerie', Amy Winehouse and Mark Ronson)

Mina
(alt. Mena)
German, meaning 'love'.

Mindy
(alt. Mindi)
Latin, meaning 'honey'.

Minerva
Roman, from the goddess of the same name.

Ming
Chinese, meaning 'bright'.

Minna
German, meaning 'helmet'.

Minnie
German, meaning 'helmet'. Often associated with the Disney character Minnie Mouse.

Mira
Latin, meaning 'admirable'.

Mirabel
(alt. Mirabella, Mirabelle)
Latin, meaning 'wonderful'.

Miranda
(alt. Meranda)
Latin, meaning 'admirable'.

Mirella
(alt. Mireille, Mirela)
Latin, meaning 'admirable'.

Miriam
Hebrew, meaning 'bitter'.

Mirta
Spanish, meaning 'crown of thorns'.

Missy
Shortened form of Melissa, meaning 'bee'.

Misty
(alt. Misti)
English, meaning 'mist'.

Mitzi
German, meaning 'bitter'.

Miu
Japanese, meaning 'beautiful feather'.

Moira
(alt. Maira)
Irish, meaning 'bitter'.

309

Molly
(alt. Mollie)
American, meaning 'bitter'.

Mona
Irish Gaelic, meaning 'aristocratic'.

Monica
(alt. Monika, Monique)
Latin, meaning 'adviser'.

Monroe
Gaelic, meaning 'mouth of the river Rotha'.

Montserrat
(alt. Monserrate)
Spanish, from the town of the same name.

Morag
Scottish, meaning 'star of the sea'.

Morgan
(alt. Morgann)
Welsh, meaning 'great and bright'.

Moriah
Hebrew, meaning 'the Lord is my teacher'.

Morwenna
Welsh, meaning 'maiden'.

Moselle
(alt. Mozell, Mozella, Mozelle)
Hebrew, meaning 'saviour'.

Mulan
Chinese, meaning 'wood orchid'.

Munin
Scandinavian, meaning 'good memory'.

Muriel
Irish Gaelic, meaning 'sea-bright'.

Mya
(alt. Myah)
Greek, meaning 'mother'.

Myfanwy
Welsh, meaning 'my little lovely one'.

Myra
Latin, meaning 'scented oil'.

Myrna
(alt. Mirna)
Irish Gaelic, meaning 'tender and beloved'.

Myrtle
Irish, from the shrub of the same name.

 Girls' names

Nadia
(alt. Nadya)
Russian, meaning 'hope'.

Nadine
French, meaning 'hope'.

Nahara
Aramaic, meaning 'light'.

Naima
Arabic, meaning 'water nymph'.

Nakia
Egyptian, meaning 'pure'.

Nalani
Hawaiian, meaning 'serenity of the skies'.

Nan
(alt. Nanna, Nannie)
Hebrew, meaning 'grace'.

Nancy
(alt. Nanci, Nancie)
Hebrew, meaning 'grace'.

Nanette
(alt. Nannette)
French, meaning 'grace'.

Naomi
(alt. Naoma, Noemi)
Hebrew, meaning 'pleasant'.

Narcissa
Greek, meaning 'daffodil'.

Nastasia

Greek, meaning 'resurrection'.

Natalie

(alt. Natalee, Natalia, Natalya, Nathalie)

Latin, meaning 'birth day'.

Natasha

(alt. Natasa)

Russian, meaning 'birth day'.

Natividad

Spanish, meaning 'Christmas'.

Neda

English, meaning 'wealthy'.

Nedra

English, meaning 'underground'.

Neema

Swahili, meaning 'born of prosperity'.

Neka

Native American, meaning 'goose'.

Nell

(alt. Nelda, Nell, Nella, Nellie, Nelly)

Shortened form of Eleanor, meaning 'light'.

Nemi

Italian, from the lake of the same name.

Neoma

Greek, meaning 'new moon'.

Nereida

Spanish, meaning 'sea nymph'.

Nerissa

Greek, meaning 'sea nymph'.

Nettie

(alt. Neta)

Shortened form of Henrietta, meaning 'ruler of the house'.

Neva

Spanish, meaning 'snowy'.

Nevaeh

American, meaning 'heaven'.

Nhung

Vietnamese, meaning 'velvet'.

Niamh
(alt. Neve)
Irish, meaning 'brightness'.

Nicki
(alt. Nicky, Nikki)
Shortened form of Nicola, meaning 'victory of the people'.

Nicola
Greek, meaning 'victory of the people'.

Nicole
(alt. Nichol, Nichole, Nicolette, Nicolle, Nikole)
Greek, meaning 'victory of the people'.

Nidia
Spanish, meaning 'graceful'.

Nigella
Irish Gaelic, meaning 'champion'.

Nikita
Greek, meaning 'unconquered'.

Nila
Egyptian, meaning 'Nile'.

Nilda
German, meaning 'battle woman'.

Nimra
Arabic, meaning 'number'.

Nina
Spanish, meaning 'girl'.

Nissa
Hebrew, meaning 'sign'.

Nita
Spanish, meaning 'gracious'.

Nixie
German, meaning 'water sprite'.

Noel
(alt. Noelle)
French, meaning 'Christmas'.

Nola
Irish Gaelic, meaning 'white shoulder'.

Nona
Latin, meaning 'ninth'.

313

Nora
(alt. Norah)
Shortened form of Eleanor, meaning 'light'.

Noreen
(alt. Norine)
Irish, meaning 'light'.

Norma
Latin, meaning 'pattern'.

Normandie
(alt. Normandy)
French, from the province of the same name.

Novia
Latin, meaning 'new'.

Nuala
Irish Gaelic, meaning 'white shoulder'.

Nydia
Latin, meaning 'nest'.

Nyimbo
Swahili, meaning 'song'.

Nysa
(alt. Nyssa)
Greek, meaning 'ambition'.

Names of goddesses

Aphrodite (Love: Greek)
Ceres (Agriculture: Roman)
Eos (Dawn: Greek)
Hestia (Hearth: Greek)
Kali (Death: Indian)
Lucinda (Childbirth: Roman)
Minerva (Wisdom: Roman)
Nephthys (Death: Egyptian)
Sesheta (Stars: Egyptian)
Terra (Earth: Roman)

N

Girls' names

Oceana
(alt. Ocean, Océane, Ocie)
Greek, meaning 'ocean'.

Octavia
Latin, meaning 'eighth'.

Oda
(alt. Odie)
Shortened form of Odessa,
meaning 'long voyage'.

Odele
(alt. Odell)
English, meaning 'woad hill'.

Odelia
Hebrew, meaning 'I will praise
the Lord'.

Odessa
Greek, meaning 'long voyage'.

Odette
(alt. Odetta)
French, meaning 'wealthy'.

Odile
(alt. Odilia)
French, meaning 'prospers in
battle'.

Odina
Feminine form of Odin, from
the Nordic god of the same
name, meaning 'creative
inspiration'.

Odyssey
Greek, meaning 'long journey'.

Oksana

Russian, meaning 'praise to God'.

Ola

(alt. Olie)

Greek, meaning 'man's defender'.

Olena

(alt. Olene)

Russian, meaning 'light'.

Olga

Russian, meaning 'holy'.

Oliana

American, meaning 'the Lord has answered'.

Olivia

(alt. Olivev, Oliviana, Olivié)

Latin, meaning 'olive'. The UK's most popular girls' name in 2011.

Ollie

Shortened form of Olivia, meaning 'olive'.

Olwen

Welsh, meaning 'white footprint'.

Olympia

(alt. Olimpia)

Greek, meaning 'from Mount Olympus'.

Oma

(alt. Omie)

Arabic, meaning 'leader'.

Omyra

Latin, meaning 'scented oil'.

Ona

(alt. Onnie)

Shortened form of Oneida, meaning 'long awaited'.

Ondine

French, meaning 'wave of water'.

Oneida

Native American, meaning 'long awaited'.

Onyx

Latin, meaning 'veined gem'.

Oona

Irish, meaning 'unity'.

Opal

Sanskrit, meaning 'gem'.

Ophelia

(alt. Ofelia, Ophélie)

Greek, meaning 'help'. Best known from Shakespeare's play *Hamlet*.

Oprah

Hebrew, meaning 'young deer'. Most often associated with Oprah Winfrey.

Ora

Latin, meaning 'prayer'.

Orabela

Latin, meaning 'prayer'.

Colour names

Azure
Cinnabar
Ebony
Fuchsia
Ivory
Olive
Rose
Saffron
Sienna
Violet

Oralie

(alt. Oralia)

French, meaning 'golden'.

Orane

French, meaning 'rising'.

Orchid

Greek, from the flower of the same name.

Oriana

(alt. Oriane)

Latin, meaning 'dawning'.

Orla

(alt. Orlaith, Orly)

Irish Gaelic, meaning 'golden lady'.

Orlean

French, meaning 'plum'.

Ornelia

Italian, meaning 'flowering ash tree'.

Orsa

(alt. Osia, Ossie)

Latin, meaning 'bear'.

Otthid

Greek, meaning 'prospers in battle'.

Ottilie
(alt. Ottie)

French, meaning 'prospers in battle'.

Ouida

French, meaning 'renowned in battle'.

Oyintsa

Native American, meaning 'white duck'.

Ozette

Native American, from the village of the same name.

Popular North American names

Abigail	Isabella
Ava	Madison
Chloe	Mia
Emily	Olivia
Emma	Sophia

Girls' names

Pacifica
(alt. Pacifika)

Spanish, meaning 'peaceful'.

Padma
Sanskrit, meaning 'lotus'.

Paige
(alt. Page)

French, meaning 'serving boy'.

Paisley
Scottish, from the town of the same name.

Palma
(alt. Palmira)

Latin, meaning 'palm tree'.

Paloma
Spanish, meaning 'dove'.

Pam
Shortened form of Pamela, meaning 'all honey'.

Pamela
(alt. Pamala, Pamella, Pamla)

Greek, meaning 'all honey'.

Pandora
Greek, meaning 'all gifted'. Also from the Greek myth.

Pangiota
Greek, meaning 'all is holy'.

Paniz
Persian, meaning 'candy'.

Pansy
French, from the flower of the same name.

Paprika

English, meaning 'spice'.

Paradisa

(alt. Paradis)

Greek, meaning 'garden orchard'.

Paris

(alt. Parisa)

Greek, from the mythological hero of the same name. Also from the city.

Parker

English, meaning 'park keeper'.

Parthenia

Greek, meaning 'virginal'.

Parthenope

Greek, from the mythological Siren of the same name.

Parvati

Sanskrit, meaning 'daughter of the mountain'.

Pascale

French, meaning 'Easter'.

Pat

(alt. Patsy, Patti, Pattie, Patty)

Shortened form of Patricia, meaning 'noble'.

Patience

French, meaning 'the state of being patient'.

Patricia

(alt. Patrice)

Latin, meaning 'noble'.

Paula

Latin, meaning 'small'.

Pauline

(alt. Paulette, Paulina)

Latin, meaning 'small'.

Paxton

Latin, meaning 'peaceful town'.

Paz

Spanish, meaning 'peace'.

Pazia

Hebrew, meaning 'golden'.

Peace

English, meaning 'peace'.

Gem and precious stone names

Amber
Beryl
Coral
Esmerelda
Jade
Marjorie
Pearl
Ruby
Topaz

Peaches

English, meaning 'peaches'.

Pearl
(alt. Pearle, Pearlie, Perla)

Latin, meaning 'pale gemstone'.

Peggy
(alt. Peggie)

Greek, meaning 'pearl'.

Pelia

Hebrew, meaning 'marvel of God'.

Penelope

Greek, meaning 'bobbin worker'.

Penny
(alt. Penni, Pennie)

Greek, meaning 'bobbin worker'.

Peony

Greek, from the flower of the same name.

Perdita

Latin, meaning 'lost'.

Peri
(alt. Perri)

Hebrew, meaning 'outcome'.

Perry

French, meaning 'pear tree'.

Persephone

Greek, meaning 'bringer of destruction'.

Petra
(alt. Petrina)

Greek, meaning 'rock'.

Petula

Latin, meaning 'to seek'.

Petunia
Greek, from the flower of the same name.

Phaedra
Greek, meaning 'bright'.

Philippa
Greek, meaning 'horse lover'.

Philomena
(alt. Philoma)
Greek, meaning 'loved one'.

Phoebe
Greek, meaning 'shining and brilliant'.

Phoenix
Greek, meaning 'red as blood'. Also from the mythical bird.

Phyllida
Greek, meaning 'leafy bough'.

Phyllis
(alt. Phillia, Phylis)
Greek, meaning 'leafy bough'.

Pia
Latin, meaning 'pious'.

Piera
Italian, meaning 'rock'.

Pilar
Spanish, meaning 'pillar'.

Piper
English, meaning 'pipe player'.

Pippa
Shortened form of Philippa, meaning 'horse lover'.

Popular Asian names

Amaya	Kai
Aoi	Miya
Hana	Murasaki
Hiro	Niu
Iku	Rei

P

Plum

Latin, from the fruit of the same name.

Polly

Hebrew, meaning 'bitter'.

Pomona

Latin, meaning 'apple'.

Poppy

Latin, from the flower of the same name.

Portia

(alt. Porsha)

Latin, meaning 'from the Portia clan'.

Posy

English, meaning 'small flower'.

Precious

Latin, meaning 'of great worth'.

Priela

Hebrew, meaning 'fruit of God'.

Primavera

Spanish, meaning 'springtime'.

Primrose

English, meaning 'first rose'.

Princess

English, meaning 'daughter of the monarch'.

Priscilla

(alt. Prisca, Priscila)

Latin, meaning 'ancient'.

Priya

Hindi, meaning 'loved one'.

Prudence

Latin, meaning 'caution'.

Prudie

Shortened form of Prudence, meaning 'caution'.

Prunella

Latin, meaning 'small plum'.

Psyche

Greek, meaning 'breath'. Also from Greek mythology and psychological theory.

Names with positive meanings

Allegra – cheerful
Augusta – magnificent
Felicia – lucky
Gladys – glad
Hilary – cheerful

Lucy – light
Phoebe – radiant
Rinah – joyful
Thalia – flourishing
Yoko – positive

 Girls' names

Qiana
(alt. Qianah, Qiania, Qyana, Qianne)
American, meaning 'gracious'.

Qiturah
Arabic, meaning 'incense'.

Queen
(alt. Queenie)
English, meaning 'queen'.

Quiana
American, meaning 'silky'.

Quincy
(alt. Quincey)
French, meaning 'estate of the fifth son'.

Quinn
Irish Gaelic, meaning 'counsel'.

Quintessa
Latin, meaning 'creative'.

Foreign alternatives

Emily – Emilie, Emeline
Helen – Galina, Helene
Mary – Marie, Maria, Marjan
Sarah – Sara, Sarine, Zara
Violet – Iolanthe, Yolanda

Palindrome names

Aja	Ette
Anna	Eve
Anona	Hannah
Elle	Ono
Emme	Viv

 Girls' names

Rachel
(alt. Rachael, Rachelle)
Hebrew, meaning 'ewe'.

Radhika
Sanskrit, meaning 'prosperous'.

Rae
(alt. Ray)
Shortened form of Rachel,
meaning 'ewe'.

Rafferty
Irish, meaning 'abundance'.

Rahima
Arabic, meaning
'compassionate'.

Raina
(alt. Rain, Raine, Rainey, Rayne)
Latin, meaning 'queen'.

Raissa
(alt. Raisa)
Yiddish, meaning 'rose'.

Raleigh
(alt. Rayleigh)
English, meaning 'meadow of
roe deer'.

Rama
(alt. Ramey, Ramya)
Hebrew, meaning 'exalted'.

Ramona
(alt. Romona)
Spanish, meaning 'wise
guardian'.

Ramsey
English, meaning 'raven island'.

Rana
(alt. *Rania, Rayna*)

Arabic, meaning 'beautiful thing'.

Randy
(alt. *Randi*)

Shortened form of Miranda, meaning 'admirable'.

Rani
Sanskrit, meaning 'queen'.

Raphaela
(alt. *Rafaela, Raffaella*)

Spanish, meaning 'healing God'.

Raquel
(alt. *Racquel*)

Hebrew, meaning 'ewe'.

Rashida
Turkish, meaning 'righteous'.

Raven
(alt. *Ravyn*)

English, from the bird of the same name.

Razia
Arabic, meaning 'contented'.

Reagan
(alt. *Reagen, Regan*)

Irish Gaelic, meaning 'descendant of Riagán'.

Reba
Shortened form of Rebecca, meaning 'joined'.

Rebecca
(alt. *Rebekah*)

Hebrew, meaning 'joined'.

Reese
Welsh, meaning 'fiery and zealous'.

Regina
Latin, meaning 'queen'.

Reiko
Japanese, meaning 'thankful one'.

Reina
(alt. *Reyna, Rheyna*)

Spanish, meaning 'queen'.

Rena
(alt. *Reena*)

Hebrew, meaning 'serene'.

Renata

Latin, meaning 'reborn'.

Rene

Greek, meaning 'peace'.

Renée
(alt. Renae)
French, meaning 'reborn'.

Renita

Latin, meaning 'resistant'.

Reshma
(alt. Resha)
Sanskrit, meaning 'silk'.

Reta
(alt. Retha, Retta)
Shortened form of Margaret, meaning 'pearl'.

Rhea

Greek, meaning 'earth'.

Rheta

Greek, meaning 'eloquent speaker'.

Rhiannon
(alt. Reanna, Reanne, Rhian, Rhianna)
Welsh, meaning 'witch'.

Rhoda

Greek, meaning 'rose'.

Rhona

Nordic, meaning 'rough island'.

Rhonda
(alt. Ronda)
Welsh, meaning 'noisy'.

Rīa
(alt. Rie, Riya)
Shortened form of Victoria, meaning 'victor'.

Ricki
(alt. Rieko, Rika, Rikki)
Shortened form of Frederica, meaning 'peaceful ruler'.

Riley

Irish Gaelic, meaning 'courageous'.

Rilla

German, meaning 'small brook'.

Rima

Arabic, meaning 'antelope'.

Riona

Irish Gaelic, meaning 'like a queen'.

Ripley

English, meaning 'shouting man's meadow'.

Risa

Latin, meaning 'laughter'.

Rita

Shortened form of Margaret, meaning 'pearl'.

River

(alt. Riviera)

English, from the body of water of the same name.

Robbie

(alt. Robi, Roby)

Shortened form of Roberta, meaning 'bright fame'.

Roberta

English, meaning 'bright fame'.

Robin

(alt. Robbin, Robyn)

English, meaning 'bright fame'.

Rochelle

(alt. Richelle, Rochel)

French, meaning 'little rock'.

Rogue

French, meaning 'beggar'.

Rohina

(alt. Rohini)

Sanskrit, meaning 'sandalwood'.

Roja

Spanish, meaning 'red-haired lady'.

Roisin

Irish Gaelic, meaning 'little rose'.

Rolanda

German, meaning 'famous land'.

Roma

Italian, meaning 'Rome'.

Romaine

(alt. Romina)

French, meaning 'from Rome'.

'Powerful' names

Adira
Edrea
Isis
Ricarda
Roxie
Ulrika

Romola
(alt. Romilda, Romily)

Latin, meaning 'Roman woman'.

Romy

Shortened form of Rosemary, meaning 'dew of the sea'.

Rona
(alt. Ronia, Ronja, Ronna)

Nordic, meaning 'rough island'.

Ronnie
(alt. Roni)

English, meaning 'strong counsel'.

Roro

Indonesian, meaning 'nobility'.

Rosa

Italian, meaning 'rose'.

Rosabel
(alt. Rosabella)

Contraction of Rose and Belle, meaning 'beautiful rose'.

Rosalie
(alt. Rosale, Rosalia, Rosalina)

French, meaning 'rose garden'.

Rosalind
(alt. Rosalinda)

Spanish, meaning 'pretty rose'.

Rosalyn
(alt. Rosaleen, Rosaline, Roselyn)

Contraction of Rose and Lynn, meaning 'pretty rose'.

Rosamond
(alt. Rosamund)

German, meaning 'renowned protector'.

Rose

Latin, from the flower of the same name.

R

Roseanne

(alt. Rosana, Rosann, Rosanna, Rosanne, Roseann, Roseanna)

Contraction of Rose and Anne, meaning 'graceful rose'.

Rosemary

(alt. Rosemarie)

Latin, meaning 'dew of the sea'.

Rosie

(alt. Rosia)

Shortened form of Rosemary, meaning 'dew of the sea'.

Rosita

Spanish, meaning 'rose'.

Rowena

(alt. Rowan)

Welsh, meaning 'slender and fair'.

Roxanne

(alt. Roxana, Roxane, Roxanna)

Persian, meaning 'dawn'.

Roxie

Shortened form of Roxanne, meaning 'dawn'.

Rubena

(alt. Rubina)

Hebrew, meaning 'behold, a son'.

Ruby

(alt. Rubi, Rubie)

English, meaning 'red gemstone'.

Rusty

American, meaning 'red-headed'.

Ruth

(alt. Ruthe, Ruthie)

Hebrew, meaning 'friend and companion'.

Popular Irish names

Aoife
Bree
Caitlin
Ciara
Eilis
Molly
Niamh
Orlaith
Shannon
Sinead

R

 Girls' names

Saba
(alt. Sabah)
Greek, meaning 'from Sheba'.

Sabina
(alt. Sabine)
Latin, meaning 'from the Sabine tribe'.

Sabrina
Latin, meaning 'the River Severn'.

Sadella
American, meaning 'fairytale princess'.

Sadie
(alt. Sade, Sadye)
Hebrew, meaning 'princess'.

Saffron
English, from the spice of the same name.

Safiya
Arabic, meaning 'sincere friend'.

Sage
(alt. Saga, Saige)
Latin, meaning 'wise and healthy'.

Sahara
Arabic, meaning 'desert'.

Sakura
Japanese, meaning 'cherry blossom'.

Sally
(alt. Sallie)
Hebrew, meaning 'princess'.

Salome
(alt. Salma)
Hebrew, meaning 'peace'.

Sam
(alt. Sammie, Sammy)
Shortened form of Samantha, meaning 'told by God'.

Samantha
Hebrew, meaning 'told by God'.

Samara
(alt. Samaria, Samira)
Hebrew, meaning 'under God's rule'.

Sanaa
Arabic, meaning 'brilliance'.

Sandra
(alt. Saundra)
Shortened form of Alexandra, meaning 'defender of mankind'.

Sandy
(alt. Sandi)
Shortened form of Sandra, meaning 'defender of mankind'.

Sangeeta
Hindi, meaning 'musical'.

Sanna
(alt. Saniya, Sanne, Sanni)
Hebrew, meaning 'lily'.

Santana
(alt. Santina)
Spanish, meaning 'holy'.

Saoirse
Irish, meaning 'freedom'.

Sapphire
(alt. Saphira)
Hebrew, meaning 'blue gemstone'.

Sarah
(alt. Sara, Sarai, Sariah)
Hebrew, meaning 'princess'.

Sasha
(alt. Sacha, Sascha)
Russian, meaning 'man's defender'.

S

Saskia
(alt. Saskie)
Dutch, meaning 'the Saxon people'.

Savannah
(alt. Savanah, Savanna, Savina)
Spanish, meaning 'treeless'.

Scarlett
(alt. Scarlet)
English, meaning 'scarlet'.

Scout
French, meaning 'to listen'.

Sedona
(alt. Sedna)
Spanish, from the city of the same name.

Selah
(alt Sela)
Hebrew, meaning 'cliff'.

Selby
English, meaning 'manor village'.

Selena
(alt. Salena, Salima, Salina, Selene, Selina)
Greek, meaning 'moon goddess'.

Selma
German, meaning 'Godly helmet'.

Seneca
Native American, meaning 'from the Seneca tribe'.

Sephora
Hebrew, meaning 'bird'.

September
Latin, meaning 'seventh month'.

Seraphina
(alt. Serafina, Seraphia, Seraphine)
Hebrew, meaning 'ardent'.

Serena
(alt. Sarina, Sereana)
Latin, meaning 'tranquil'.

Serenity
Latin, meaning 'serene'.

Shania
(alt. Shaina, Shana, Shaniya)
Hebrew, meaning 'beautiful'.

S

Shanice

American, meaning 'from Africa'.

Shaniqua

(alt. Shanika)

African, meaning 'warrior princess'.

Shanna

English, meaning 'old'.

Shannon

(alt. Shannan, Shanon)

Irish Gaelic, meaning 'old and ancient'.

Shantal

(alt. Shantel, Shantell)

French, meaning 'stone'.

Shanti

Hindi, meaning 'peaceful'.

Sharlene

German, meaning 'man'.

Sharon

(alt. Sharen, Sharona, Sharron, Sharyn)

Hebrew, meaning 'a plain'.

Nautical names

Coral
Halimedi
Marina
Nereida
Sagara

Shasta

American, from the mountain of the same name.

Shauna

(alt. Shawna)

Irish, meaning 'the Lord is gracious'.

Shayla

(alt. Shaylie, Shayna, Sheyla)

Irish, meaning 'blind'.

Shea

Irish Gaelic, meaning 'from the fairy fort'.

Sheena

Irish, meaning 'the Lord is gracious'.

S

Sheila
(alt. Shelia)
Irish, meaning 'blind'.

Shelby
(alt. Shelba, Shelbie)
English, meaning 'estate on the ledge'.

Shelley
(alt. Shelli, Shellie, Shelly)
English, meaning 'meadow on the ledge'.

Shenandoah
Native American, meaning 'after an Oneida chief'.

Sheridan
Irish Gaelic, meaning 'wild man'.

Sherry
(alt. Sheree, Sheri, Sherie, Sherri, Sherrie)
Shortened form of Cheryl, meaning 'man'.

Sheryl
(alt. Sherryl)
German, meaning 'man'.

Shiloh
Hebrew, meaning 'his gift'. From the biblical place of the same name.

Shirley
(alt. Shirlee)
English, meaning 'bright meadow'.

Shivani
Sanskrit, meaning 'wife of Shiva'.

Shona
Irish Gaelic, meaning 'God is gracious'.

Shoshana
(alt. Shoshanna)
Hebrew, meaning 'lily'.

Shura
Russian, meaning 'man's defender'.

Sian
(alt. Sianna)
Welsh, meaning 'the Lord is gracious'.

Sibyl
(alt. Sybil)
Greek, meaning 'seer and oracle'.

Sidney
(alt. Sydney)
English, meaning 'from St Denis'.

Sidonie
(alt. Sidonia, Sidony)
Latin, meaning 'from Sidonia'.

Siena
(alt. Sienna)
Latin, from the town of the same name.

Sierra
Spanish, meaning 'saw'.

Siffhi
Hindi, meaning 'spiritual powers'.

Signa
(alt. Signe)
Scandinavian, meaning 'victory'.

Sigrid
Nordic, meaning 'fair victory'.

Silja
Scandinavian, meaning 'blind'.

Simcha
Hebrew, meaning 'joy'.

Simone
(alt. Simona)
Hebrew, meaning 'listening intently'.

Sinead
Irish, meaning 'the Lord is gracious'.

Siobhan
Irish, meaning 'the Lord is gracious'.

Siren
(alt. Sirena)
Greek, meaning 'entangler'.

Siria
Spanish, meaning 'glowing'.

Sisika
Native American, meaning 'like a bird'.

Skye
(alt. Sky)
Scottish, from the island of the same name.

Skyler
(alt. Skyla, Skylar)
Dutch, meaning 'giving shelter'.

Sloane
(alt. Sloan)
Irish Gaelic, meaning 'man of arms'.

Socorro
Spanish, meaning 'to aid'.

Sojourner
English, meaning 'temporary stay'.

Solana
Spanish, meaning 'sunlight'.

Solange
French, meaning 'with dignity'.

Soledad
Spanish, meaning 'solitude'.

Soleil
French, meaning 'sun'.

Solveig
Scandinavian, meaning 'woman of the house'.

Sona
Arabic, meaning 'golden one'.

Sonia
(alt. Sonja, Sonya)
Greek, meaning 'wisdom'.

Sophia
(alt. Sofia, Sofie, Sophie)
Greek, meaning 'wisdom'.

Sophronia
Greek, meaning 'sensible'.

Soraya
Persian, meaning 'princess'.

Sorcha
Irish Gaelic, meaning 'bright and shining'.

Sorrel
English, from the herb of the same name.

Stacey
(alt. Stacie, Stacy)
Greek, meaning 'resurrection'.

Star
(alt. Starla, Starr)
English, meaning 'star'.

Stella
Latin, meaning 'star'.

Stephanie
(alt. Stefanie, Stephani, Stephania, Stephany)
Greek, meaning 'crowned'.

Sue
(alt. Susie, Suzy)
Shortened form of Susan, meaning 'lily'.

Sukey
(alt. Sukey, Sukie)
Shortened form of Susan, meaning 'lily'.

Summer
English, from the season of the same name.

Sunday
English, meaning 'the first day'.

Sunny
(alt. Sun)
English, meaning 'of a pleasant temperament'.

Suri
Persian, meaning 'red rose'.

Surya
Hindi, from the god of the same name.

Susan
(alt. Susann, Suzan)
Hebrew, meaning 'lily'.

Susannah
(alt. Susana, Susanna, Susanne, Suzanna, Suzanne)
Hebrew, meaning 'lily'.

Svea
Swedish, meaning 'of the motherland'.

Svetlana
Russian, meaning 'star'.

Swanhild
Saxon, meaning 'battle swan'.

Sylvia
(alt. Silvia, Sylvie)
Latin, meaning 'from the forest'.

 Girls' names

Tabitha
(alt. Tabatha)
Aramaic, meaning 'gazelle'.

Tahira
Arabic, meaning 'virginal'.

Tai
Chinese, meaning 'big'.

Taima
(alt. Taina)
Native American, meaning 'peal of thunder'.

Tajsa
Polish, meaning 'princess'.

Talia
(alt. Tali)
Hebrew, meaning 'heaven's dew'.

Taliesin
Welsh, meaning 'shining brow'.

Talise
(alt. Talyse)
Native American, meaning 'lovely water'.

Talitha
Aramaic, meaning 'young girl'.

Tallulah
(alt. Taliyah)
Native American, meaning 'leaping water'.

Tamara
(alt. Tamera)
Hebrew, meaning 'palm tree'.

Famous artists

Barbara (Hepworth)
Bridget (Riley)
Louise (Bourgeois)
Tracey (Emin)
Yoko (Ono)

Tamatha
(alt. Tametha)

American, meaning 'dear Tammy'.

Tamika
(alt. Tameka)

American, meaning 'people'.

Tammy
(alt. Tami, Tammie)

Shortened form of Tamsin, meaning 'twin'.

Tamsin

Hebrew, meaning 'twin'.

Tanis

Spanish, meaning 'to make famous'.

Tanya
(alt. Tania, Tanya, Tonya)

Shortened form of Tatiana, meaning 'from the Tatius clan'.

Tao

Chinese, meaning 'like a peach'.

Tara
(alt. Tarah, Tera)

Irish Gaelic, meaning 'rocky hill'.

Tasha
(alt. Taisha, Tarsha)

Shortened form of Natasha, meaning 'Christmas'.

Tatiana
(alt. Tayana)

Russian, meaning 'from the Tatius clan'.

Tatum

English, meaning 'light hearted'.

Tawny
(alt. Tawanaa, Tawnee, Tawnya)

English, meaning 'golden brown'.

Taya

Greek, meaning 'poor one'.

Taylor
(alt. Tayler)

English, meaning 'tailor'.

Tea

Greek, meaning 'goddess'.

Teagan
(alt. Teague, Tegan)

Irish Gaelic, meaning 'poet'.

Teal

English, from the bird of the same name.

Tecla

Greek, meaning 'fame of God'.

Tehile

Hebrew, meaning 'song of praise'.

Temperance

English, meaning 'virtue'.

Tempest

French, meaning 'storm'.

Teresa
(alt. Terese, Tereza, Theresa, Therese)

Greek, meaning 'harvest'.

Terry
(alt. Teri, Terrie)

Shortened form of Teresa, meaning 'harvest'.

Tessa
(alt. Tess, Tessie)

Shortened form of Teresa, meaning 'harvest'.

Thais

Greek, from the mythological heroine of the same name.

Thalia

Greek, meaning 'blooming'.

Thandi
(alt. Thana)

Arabic, meaning 'thanksgiving'.

Thea

Greek, meaning 'goddess'.

Theda

German, meaning 'people'.

Thelma

Greek, meaning 'will'.

Theodora

Greek, meaning 'gift of God'.

Theodosia

Greek, meaning 'gift of God'.

Thisbe

Greek, from the mythological heroine of the same name.

Thomasina

(alt. Thomasin, Thomasine, Thomasyn)

Greek, meaning 'twin'.

Thora

Scandinavian, meaning 'Thor's struggle'.

Tia

(alt. Tiana)

Spanish, meaning 'aunt'.

Tiara

Latin, meaning 'jewelled headband'.

Tien

Vietnamese, meaning 'fairy child'.

Tierney

Irish Gaelic, meaning 'Lord'.

Tierra

(alt. Tiera)

Spanish, meaning 'land'.

Tiffany

(alt. Tiffani, Tiffanie)

Greek, meaning 'God's appearance'.

Tiggy

Shortened form of Tigris, meaning 'tiger'.

Tigris

Irish Gaelic, meaning 'tiger'.

Tilda

Shortened form of Matilda, meaning 'battle-mighty'.

Tillie

(alt. Tilly)

Shortened form of Matilda, meaning 'battle-mighty'.

Timothea

Greek, meaning 'honouring God'.

T

Tina
(alt. Teena, Tena)

Shortened form of Christina, meaning 'anointed Christian'.

Tirion

Welsh, meaning 'kind and gentle'.

Tirzah

Hebrew, meaning 'pleasantness'.

Titania

Greek, meaning 'giant'.

Toby
(alt. Tobi)

Hebrew, meaning 'God is good'.

Tomoko

Japanese, meaning 'intelligent'.

Toni
(alt. Tony)

Latin, meaning 'invaluable'.

Tonia
(alt. Tonja, Tonya)

Russian, meaning 'praiseworthy'.

Topaz

Latin, meaning 'golden gemstone'.

Tori
(alt. Tora)

Shortened form of Victoria, meaning 'victory'.

Tova
(alt. Tovah, Tove)

Hebrew, meaning 'good'.

Tracy
(alt. Tracey, Tracie)

Greek, meaning 'harvest'.

Treva

Welsh, meaning 'homestead'.

Tricia

Shortened form of Patricia, meaning 'aristocratic'.

Autumn names

Aeria
Axelle
Peace
Shanti
Zulma

345

Trilby

English, meaning 'vocal trills'.
Also a kind of hat.

Trina

(alt. Trena)

Greek, meaning 'pure'.

Trinity

Latin, meaning 'triad'.

Trisha

Shortened form of Patricia,
meaning 'noble'.

Trista

Latin, meaning 'sad'.

Trixie

Shortened form of Beatrix,
meaning 'bringer of gladness'.

Trudy

(alt. Tru, Trudie)

Shortened form of Gertrude,
meaning 'strength of a spear'.

Tullia

Spanish, meaning 'bound for
glory'.

Tunder

Hungarian, meaning 'fairy'.

Twyla

(alt. Twila)

American, meaning 'star'.

Tyler

English, meaning 'tiler'.

Tyra

Scandinavian, meaning 'Thor's
struggle'.

Tzipporah

Hebrew, meaning 'bird'.

Popular Scottish names

Alana
Catriona
Elsie
Elspeth
Flora
Heather
Isla
Kirsty
Morag
Rhona

T

 Girls' names

Udaya

Indian, meaning 'dawn'.

Ula
(alt. Ulla)

Celtic, meaning 'gem of the sea'.

Ulrika
(alt. Urica)

German, meaning 'power of the wolf'.

Uma

Sanskrit, meaning 'flax'.

Una

Latin, meaning 'one'.

Undine

Latin, meaning 'little wave'.

Famous athletes

Denise (Lewis)
Kelly (Holmes)
Mary (Rand)
Paula (Radcliffe)
Sally (Gunnell)

Unice

Greek, meaning 'victorious'.

Unique

Latin, meaning 'only one'.

Unity

English, meaning 'oneness'.

Uriela

Hebrew, meaning 'God's light'.

Urja
(alt. Urjitha)

Indian, meaning 'energy'.

Ursula

Latin, meaning 'little female bear'.

Uta

German, meaning 'prospers in battle'.

Popular South American names

Adriel	Frances
Albany	Lily
Carolina	Mariana
Elena	Natalia
Eréndira	Poppy

Girls' names

Vada

German, meaning 'famous ruler'.

Valdis

(alt. Valdiss, Valdys, Valdyss)

Norse, meaning 'goddess of the dead', based on the mythological goddess of the same name.

Vale

Shortened form of Valencia, meaning 'strong and healthy'.

Valencia

(alt. Valancy, Valarece)

Latin, meaning 'strong and healthy'.

Valentina

Latin, meaning 'strong and healthy'.

Valentine

Latin, from the saint of the same name.

Valeria

Latin, meaning 'to be healthy and strong'.

Valerie

(alt. Valarie, Valery, Valorie)

Latin, meaning 'to be healthy and strong'.

Valia
(alt. Vallie)

Shortened form of Valerie, meaning 'to be healthy and strong'.

Vandana

Sanskrit, meaning 'worship'.

Vanessa
(alt. Vanesa)

English, from the *Gulliver's Travels* character of the same name.

Vanetta
(alt. Vanettah, Vaneta, Vanete, Vanity)

Greek, alternative of Vanessa, meaning 'like a butterfly'.

Vanity

Latin, meaning 'self-obsessed'.

Vashti

Persian, meaning 'beauty'.

Veda

Sanskrit, meaning 'knowledge and wisdom'.

Vega

Arabic, meaning 'falling vulture'.

Velda

German, meaning 'ruler'.

Vella

American, meaning 'beautiful'.

Velma

English, meaning 'determined protector'.

Venice
(alt. Venetia, Venita)

Latin, meaning 'city of canals'. From the city of the same name.

Venus

Latin, from the Roman goddess of the same name.

Vera
(alt. Verla, Verlie)

Slavic, meaning 'faith'.

Verda
(alt. Verdie)

Latin, meaning 'spring-like'.

Christmas names

Holly
Ivy
Mary
Natalie
Robyn

Verena
Latin, meaning 'true'.

Verity
Latin, meaning 'truth'.

Verna
(alt. Vernie)
Latin, meaning 'spring green'.

Verona
Latin, shortened form of
Veronica. From the city of the
same name.

Veronica
(alt. Verica, Veronique)
Latin, meaning 'true image'.

Veruca
Latin, meaning 'wart'.

Vesta
Latin, from the Roman goddess
of the same name.

Vevina
Scottish, meaning 'pleasant
lady'.

Vicenta
Latin, meaning 'prevailing'.

Vicky
(alt. Vicki, Vickie, Vikki, Vix)
Shortened form of Victoria,
meaning 'victory'.

Victoria
Latin, meaning 'victory'.

Vida
Spanish, meaning 'life'.

Vidya
Sanskrit, meaning 'knowledge'.

Vienna
Latin, from the city of the same
name.

Vigdis
Scandinavian, meaning 'war
goddess'.

351

Vina
(alt. Vena)
Spanish, meaning 'vineyard'.

Viola
Latin, meaning 'violet'.

Violet
(alt. Violetta)
Latin, meaning 'purple'.

Virgie
Shortened form of Virginia,
meaning 'maiden'.

Virginia
(alt. Virginie)
Latin, meaning 'maiden'.

Visara
Sanskrit, meaning 'celestial'.

Vita
Latin, meaning 'life'.

Vittoria
Variation of Victoria, meaning
'victory'.

Viva
Latin, meaning 'alive'.

Viveca
Scandinavian, meaning 'war
fortress'.

Vivian
(alt. Vivien, Vivienne)
Latin, meaning 'lively'.

Vonda
Czech, meaning 'from the tribe
of Vandals'.

Food and drinks-inspired names

Anise
Brandy
Cinnamon
Coco
Ginger
Madeleine
Olive
Polenta
Saffron

 Girls' names

Waleska
Polish, meaning 'beautiful'.

Wallis
English, meaning 'from Wales'.

Walta
African, meaning 'like a shield'.

Wanda
(alt. Waneta, Wanita)
Slavic, meaning 'tribe of the vandals'.

Waneta
(alt. Wanita)
Variation of Wanda, meaning 'tribe of the vandals'.

Wanita
Variation of Wanda meaning 'tribe of the vandals'.

Wava
English, meaning 'way'.

Waverly
Old English, meaning 'meadow of aspens'.

Wendy
English, meaning 'friend'.

Wharton
English, meaning 'from the river'.

Whisper
English, meaning 'whisper'.

Whitley
Old English, meaning 'white meadow'.

353

Whitney

Old English, meaning 'white island'.

Wilda

German, meaning 'willow tree'.

Wilfreda

English, feminine form of Wilfred, meaning 'to will peace'.

Wilhelmina

German, meaning 'determined'.

Willene

(alt. Willia, Willa)

German, meaning 'helmet'.

Willow

English, from the tree of the same name.

Wilma

German, meaning 'protection'.

Winifred

Old English, meaning 'holy and blessed'.

Winnie

Shortened form of Winifred, meaning 'holy and blessed'.

Winona

(alt. Wynona)

Indian, meaning 'first born daughter'.

Winslow

English, meaning 'friend's hill'.

Winter

English, meaning 'winter'.

Wisteria

English, meaning 'flower'.

Wren

English, from the bird of the same name.

Wynda

Scottish, meaning 'of the narrow passage'.

Wynne

Welsh, meaning 'white'.

Bird names

Avis
Evelyn
Raven
Starling
Teal
Wren

 Girls' names

Xanadu
African, meaning 'of exotic paradise'.

Xanthe
Greek, meaning 'blonde'.

Xanthippe
Greek, meaning 'nagging'.

Xaverie
Greek, meaning 'bright'.

Xaviera
Arabic, meaning 'bright'.

Xena
Greek, meaning 'foreigner'.

Xenia
Greek, meaning 'foreigner'.

Ximena
Greek, meaning 'listening'.

Xiomara
Spanish, meaning 'battle-ready'.

Xiu
Chinese, meaning 'elegant'.

Xochitl
Spanish, meaning 'flower'.

Xoey
Variant of Zoe, meaning 'life'.

Xristina

Variation of Christina, meaning 'follower of Christ'.

Xylia

(alt. Xylina, Xyloma)

Greek, meaning 'from the woods'.

Popular Welsh names

Bronwen	Myfanwy
Carys/Cerys	Rhiannon
Elen	Sian
Guinevere	Tegan
Megan	Wynne

Girls' names

Yadira
Arabic, meaning 'worthy'.

Yael
Hebrew, meaning 'mountain goat'.

Yaffa
(alt. Yahaira, Yajaira)
Hebrew, meaning 'lovely'.

Yamilet
Arabic, meaning 'beautiful'.

Yana
Hebrew, meaning 'the Lord is gracious'.

Yanha
Arabic, meaning 'dovelike'.

Yanira
Hawaiian, meaning 'pretty'.

Yareli
Latin, meaning 'golden'.

Yaretzi
(alt. Yaritza)
Hawaiian, meaning 'forever beloved'.

Yasmin
(alt. Yasmeen, Yasmina)
Persian, meaning 'jasmine flower'.

Yelena
Greek, meaning 'bright and chosen'.

Yeraldina
Spanish, meaning 'ruled with a spear'.

Yesenia
Arabic, meaning 'flower'.

Yetta

English, from Henrietta, meaning 'ruler of the house'.

Yeva

Hebrew variant of Eve, meaning 'life'.

Ylva

Old Norse, meaning 'sea wolf'.

Yoki

(alt. Yoko)

Native American, meaning 'rain'.

Yolanda

(alt. Yolonda)

Spanish, meaning 'violet flower'.

Yoselin

English, meaning 'lovely'.

Yoshiko

Japanese, meaning 'good child'.

Yovela

Hebrew, meaning 'jubilee'.

Ysabel

English, meaning 'God's promise'.

Fiery names

Ardea
Blaise
Enya
Vesta

Ysanne

Contraction of Isabel and Anne, meaning 'pledged to God' and 'grace'.

Yuki

Japanese, meaning 'lucky'.

Yuliana

Latin, meaning 'youthful'.

Yuridia

Russian, meaning 'farmer'.

Yusia

Arabic, meaning 'success'.

Yvette

(alt. Yvonne)

French, meaning 'yew'.

 Girls' names

Zafira
Arabic, meaning 'successful'.

Zahara
(alt. Zahava, Zahra)
Arabic, meaning 'flowering and shining'.

Zaida
(alt. Zaide).
Arabic, meaning 'prosperous'.

Zalika
Swahili, meaning 'well born'.

Zaltana
Arabic, meaning 'high mountain'.

Zamia
Greek, meaning 'pine cone'.

Zaneta
(alt. Zanceta, Zanetah, Zanett, Zanetta)
Hebrew, meaning 'a gracious present from God'.

Zaniyah
Arabic, meaning 'lily'.

Zara
(alt. Zaria, Zariah, Zora)
Arabic, meaning 'radiance'.

Zelda
German, meaning 'dark battle'.

Zelia
(alt. Zella)
Scandinavian, meaning 'sunshine'.

Zelma

German, meaning 'helmet'.

Zemirah

Hebrew, meaning 'joyous melody'.

Zena

(alt. Zenia, Zina)

Greek, meaning 'hospitable'.

Zenaida

Greek, meaning 'the life of Zeus'.

Zenobia

Latin, meaning 'the life of Zeus'.

Zephyr

Greek, meaning 'the west wind'.

Zetta

Italian, meaning 'Z'.

Zia

Arabic, meaning 'light and splendour'.

Zinaida

Greek, meaning 'belonging to Zeus'.

Zinnia

Latin, meaning 'flower'.

Zipporah

Hebrew, meaning 'bird'.

Zita

(alt. Ziva)

Spanish, meaning 'little girl'.

Zoe

Greek, meaning 'life'.

Zoila

Greek, meaning 'life'.

Zoraida

Spanish, meaning 'captivating woman'.

Zorina

Slavic, meaning 'golden'.

Zosia

(alt. Zosima)

Greek, meaning 'wisdom'.

Zoya

Greek, meaning 'life'.

Zula

African, meaning 'brilliant'.

Zuleika

Arabic, meaning 'fair and intelligent'.

Zulma

Arabic, meaning 'peace'.

Zuzana

Hebrew, meaning 'lily'.

Zuzu

Czech, meaning 'flower'.

Popular Australian names

Amelia
Charlotte
Chloe
Ella
Emily
Isabella
Mia
Olivia
Sienna
Sophie

Z

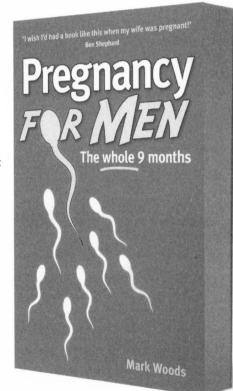